THINK *like your* DOG

And Enjoy the Rewards

Dianna M. Young with Robert H. Mottram

Island Book Publishing, LLC
PO Box 901
Anacortes, WA 98221

Order online: HowToThinkLikeYourDog.com

ISBN 13 – 978-0-9892008-0-6
Library of Congress Control Number: 2013906787

The techniques presented in this book are for informational purposes only. Each situation is unique, and a person who administers training to a canine must use appropriate discretion and good judgment. If a person lacks adequate personal experience in this endeavor, he or she should seek advice from a certified canine behaviorist, a professional trainer or another appropriate professional.

Cover design by Teri Boggs, nwgraphicdesign.com

Cover photo and interior photos by Ryan Grae Paraggio, RyanGrae.com, unless otherwise noted

Interior design by Kevin Rhoades, kevinrhoades.com

Printed in the USA.

This book is dedicated to my parents, who have supported all of my projects dating back to my earliest memories; to my husband, Jason Young, who is a terrific business partner and wonderful life partner; and to my sons, Alexander and Nicholas. May they find the same joy in dogs that their mother has found. It also is dedicated to all of my dog friends, past and present. They have been wonderful teachers.

– Dianna M. Young

Contents

Acknowledgement

Many people influence an individual for the good over the course of a lifetime, and no one has influenced my professional life more than Certified Master Trainer John M. Henkel, my teacher and mentor. It was my tremendously good fortune to work for him and apprentice with him at his canine training center in New England. I soon discovered that all my earlier studies under European master trainers and at a school for professional dog trainers in the United States were but preludes to prepare me for the things I was about to learn from John. He shared with me not only his boundless knowledge but his unlimited enthusiasm. He was not only my teacher and mentor, he was my inspiration.

– Dianna M. Young

Introduction

Almost every dog owner wants a stable, dependable canine companion to bond with in a rewarding relationship. That's a perfectly reasonable desire and a perfectly realistic one. And it's the reason for this book.

Rewarding relationships usually don't happen by accident. They happen because an owner cares enough to choose a companion wisely and then to expend the time and the patience necessary to nurture his dog's inborn ability to provide friendship and companionship. It works, because the dog-human relationship is rare in nature; two distinct species that live in exceedingly close proximity and that communicate so readily and so well with each other.

Dogs are amazingly adept at reading the subtle physical cues that we broadcast sometimes without even knowing it and that reveal so much about our state of mind. How many times have you heard a person say about her dog, "He's so amazing. He knows when I'm happy. He knows when I'm sad."

And he does, of course. Dogs know a lot about us because they are able to read us almost as well as they read other dogs.

With a little instruction, we can read them, also, which is what I intend to help you do. That skill begins with understanding how dogs think.

My first exposure to dogs on a professional level occurred in Europe, where I lived for several years in my early 20s. It was my good fortune to study there under several master trainers who shared skills that were derived from the classic dog-training traditions of the Old World. Later I continued my studies in the United States, where I learned new ways of looking at old problems and how best to find solutions for them.

Since then I have trained dogs and their handlers successfully by the many hundreds, if not by the thousands, in a variety of skills ranging from the simple to the highly complex. It has been a two-way street. These dog-and-handler teams have enhanced my education, too, by showing me clearly what works and what doesn't.

What you will find in this book is not academic theory. It is boots-on-the-ground information from a boots-on-the-ground professional trainer who has learned her craft in a painstaking way. This book is about what works and why it works. It will help to put you inside the head of your canine companion and to understand the processes that go on there. Then it will show you how to make that information work for you.

The principles that I share with you in this book, when properly applied, will reward you with a happy dog, a disciplined dog, and a fulfilling companion with whom you will be pleased to share your life. If you are a new dog owner, or simply the owner of a new dog, you are at an enviable place in life: at the start of a budding relationship and feeling the wonderful anticipation of imagining what awaits you both just a little way down the road.

I wish you and your dog the best as you travel there together.

Chapter 1
A Fundamental Truth

He is your friend, your partner, your defender, your dog. . . . He will be yours, faithful and true, to the last beat of his heart. You owe it to him to be worthy of such devotion.

– Author unknown

Many of my new training clients seek some profound insight, some magic elixir that will enable them to penetrate the mental divide that exists between human and canine. They often ask if I can identify the most important things they need to know about the way dogs think and behave, and condense them into a few simple guidelines.

My answer is, "Yes."

In fact, I can do better than that. I can boil down what they most need to know into one brief sentence that reveals a fundamental truth about human-canine dynamics. And here it is:

"In every dog-and-handler team, *without exception*, there is a leader and there is a follower."

Observe things in the context of that principle, and you will gain insights that may amaze you. It may lead to the most important discoveries you ever make about dogs and people. Utilizing this fundamental truth will dramatically increase your understanding of what plays out in front of you, and will open your eyes to important things that you may have disregarded in the past. You will become aware of nuances in human-canine interaction that you might have overlooked before. It is the foundation upon which good dog-and-handler relationships are built.

The next time you go to a friend's house and are greeted at the door by her dog's unstoppable, out-of-control barking, think about this principle. The next time a friend directs his dog to get off the furniture and the dog hesitates as if to mull the directive over, think about the principle. The next time you see a person lurch down the street with his arm outstretched, his dog straining against its leash in order to sniff this post and that bush, think about the principle.

And the next time you are approached by a handler whose dog walks calmly at his side, looking up to take direction, and then perhaps greets you calmly and politely, think about the principle.

Let me repeat it one time for emphasis:

In every dog-and-handler team, *without exception*, there is a leader and there is a follower.

The question is which is which? The dog and the handler never are equals, because in a dog's world things don't work that way. One of them is in charge of the other. Determining which is which will reveal a tremendous amount about the private lives of the dog and the person; perhaps more than the person would like.

Now you know the single most-important thing there is to know about human-canine dynamics. Keep it in mind as we proceed together through this book. It is the secret that virtually every competent professional trainer uses as a foundation for his programs.

The fact is dogs, by their nature, are rather uncomfortable until they have sorted out where they stand in a social hierarchy, whether it is a society of canines or of canines and people. When all the sorting is finished, you may emerge as the leader. If you do not, your dog will, by default, because it is hard-wired to do so.

There's nothing wrong with that, by the way, if you don't mind living in a home where many or most of the decisions are made by a dog. Some people do that.

However, if you wish to assume the leader's role in your home, I'll show you how. My job is to put you on the leadership end of the leash, and to keep you there.

Rank

Dogs are gregarious animals, as are humans. Most dogs enjoy the company of other dogs and also of humans, and derive great comfort and security from being members of a pack. This leads to their embrace of a hierarchal structure in their social arrangements, apparently in the interest of maintaining order.

Hierarchy among dogs is not as sharply defined as it is among wolves, for example, where a pack usually is an extended family, where usually only the alpha pair of wolves in a pack breeds and where other members of the pack may have to wait to eat until the leaders have finished. In the wild, the alpha wolves not only are the only breeding pair, but also are the parental figures to the rest of the pack. They take charge of security, and control all of the pack's resources, such as food and shelter. Human parents function very much the same way – taking charge of family security and apportioning resources such as food and shelter.

While different from wolves, dogs most definitely do embrace the concept of hierarchal rank, and assign rank not only to the fellow canines in their household but also to the humans. In households with male and female dogs, by the way, a matriarch most commonly leads the pack. Even in two-dog households, it is most likely a female that will be in charge, even if the female is a field spaniel and the male is a mastiff.

What information does this give us? It tells us that dogs naturally gravitate toward leader-follower roles.

Leadership

To feel secure, a dog needs to know specifically whether he is a leader or a follower. In the canine world, the biggest dog is not always the leader. The toughest dog, psychologically, usually is. In a mix of dogs of several sizes, the leader may turn out to be your 4-pound Chihuahua. That surprises people sometimes.

How do dogs determine leadership among themselves? They assert themselves through play, and under most circumstances sort themselves out that way. As dogs chase and wrestle and jump on each other, we might interpret it as no more than two dogs playing. But that doesn't accord the activity nearly the importance it is due, because much more is going on.

Determining leadership doesn't necessarily require combat. A dog can display force of personality by the way it approaches other dogs, or by the way it approaches common food bowls. It can display force of personality, or lack of it, by the kind of eye contact it makes or avoids making. It can display its leadership potential by the way it carries its ears. Are they forward and erect, or laid back and passive? And it reveals a lot through its tail. Is the tail carried up, or down?

Wagging, by the way, is irrelevant. Humans often think that a wagging dog is a friendly dog. But a dog can be excited in a negative way, and still wag his tail. A canine bully may wag his tail before a fight because he enjoys fighting.

A human takes leadership with a dog the same way another dog would; through assertive body language. In a human-canine relationship, we need not feel bashful about taking a leadership role. It is a kindness to do so, in fact, because it makes our dog feel more secure. Being hierarchal animals, they are extremely uncomfortable until they have determined the rank of everyone in the household, including themselves. They love a strong leader. A strong leader gives them warm-and-fuzzy feelings, gives them a sense of safety. Dogs also love consistent routine. It adds to their feeling of security.

Some people are strong and confident leaders by nature. Others are not, but can learn to become one through training. In canine relationships, the leader manages most activities that he or she views as important, and has final say, if he wants it, about everything that happens. The leader also controls the entire pack's security at all times. You must perform these duties satisfactorily in your family pack, because if you do not, your dog will attempt to do so. He has no choice. It is not misbehavior on his part. He is hard-wired from birth to try to fill any leadership vacuum he perceives.

A dog in a relationship with a human who does not exhibit leadership feels uncomfortable to a greater or lesser extent. A dog that is psychologically weak feels that lack the most, because a weak dog requires strong leadership. He looks for a pack mate that will make decisions for him and protect him. If that leadership entity doesn't exist, it creates insecurity, and the dog may become mildly to frantically distressed.

A strong dog will not necessarily become distressed. He will assume the leadership role himself. A problem with that is that he is likely to become increasingly overconfident in his own decisions, whether good or bad. We are concerned primarily with his bad decisions, such as those concerning home security. They will involve who and what he perceives to be a threat and what he decides to do about it.

Chapter 2
How Do Dogs Think?

Did you ever walk into a room and forget why you walked in? I think that's how dogs spend their lives.

— Sue Murphy

It often surprises people who bring their dogs to us for training, but at Camano Island Kennels we spend at least as much time training people as we do training dogs. Why? Because people don't instinctively know how to think like dogs. And if we are to succeed with dogs, we have to meet them on their own intellectual level. They cannot meet us on ours.

Obviously, dogs and people think differently because they are *wired* to think differently, something that a successful owner and trainer must overcome. Dogs cannot learn to think like people, however, so we must learn to think like dogs.

We humans often can figure out the probable outcomes of potential behaviors even though we may not actually have experienced them. We know, for example, that if we try to beat the train to the crossing too many times, it probably is going to turn our car – and us – into a pile of junk. Dogs cannot do that. Most of the things they know, they have had to learn by actual experience, and often by multiple repetitions of that experience.

For example, a dog out for a stroll on his own may come to the side of a highway, hesitate, and look both ways before he crosses the road. We might observe this and think, *Wow, what an intelligent dog. He's figured out that he has to watch for cars.* It's more likely, however, that what we see is a dog that has been lucky. Perhaps he approached a roadway in the past, stepped onto the pavement, and a speeding car blasted its horn, swerved dramatically away and threw gravel on the startled dog. This experience may have taught him to be wary of roads and vehicles.

A different dog, one that perhaps might have needed more repetitions of an experience to learn from it, may be the dead dog we have seen lying by the side of the road.

Another difference in the human and dog thought processes: Dogs live in the moment. They don't reflect back, and they don't think ahead. Your dog does not sit in front of your holiday decorations, for example, and think, *Ah, yes, I remember what I was doing last year at this time.* When your dog gets into the garbage and scatters it around the kitchen, he doesn't think, *Oh, boy, when my owner gets home, I'm really going to catch it!*

Dogs can make surprising connections, however, and here's an example of how that thought process works. Our family lives on several rural acres, surrounded by beautiful Northwest forest. We can't see people coming up our long and twisting driveway so, until recently, they sometimes arrived unexpectedly. When they did, the dogs that live with us set up a warning racket that often awakened our young children. In an effort to solve this problem, we installed an electronic monitor near the far end of the driveway that detects passing vehicles and broadcasts their presence to a speaker in the house. "Alert, Zone 1," the speaker says, and repeats the phrase two more times. We thought this would give us time to get the dogs gathered into a back room before a vehicle arrived at our door, and would eliminate a lot of barking.

What has happened instead is that now the dogs bark as soon as they hear the announcement. They have learned – through multiple repetitions – that the broadcast occurs a couple of minutes before people arrive. We would be incorrect to assume that they understand that what they hear is a driveway alarm. And they certainly do not comprehend the words that the speaker broadcasts. As far as the dogs are concerned, it might as well be saying "pepperoni pizza." But they have learned by repetition that when they hear the sound, an unknown person will arrive a couple of minutes later.

Language

What does language mean to your dog? What language does it understand? If you bought it from a kennel up the road, does it understand English? If you imported it from Frankfurt, does it understand German? Will English confuse it or upset it?

We often use language to communicate with our dogs. We create verbal commands which we expect them to learn and which we expect them to respond to correctly.

However, if we suddenly lost our ability to speak, we still could communicate just fine with our dogs. How? Through body language. In fact, body language is many times more important to our dogs than anything that comes out of our mouths.

My family and I were watching an old movie on TV one night that dramatically illustrated a misconception that many people have about canine communications. The movie was about a cute little canine rascal who had a knack for getting himself and his friends into dangerous situations and then getting them out again. One of the characters in the movie was the canine star's doggie girlfriend.

At one point, the canine couple needed to venture on a mission into an apparently haunted house, but first they needed to exchange some information. So the diminutive doggy hero asked his girlfriend a question. "Woof, woof, woof, woof?" he barked. "Woof, woof!" she replied.

Movies like that are adorable, but they don't help us improve our understanding of how dogs communicate. This is not to say that dogs never vocalize. Dogs will sound an alert when a strange car comes up the driveway, which advises other dogs on the property that a potential stranger is approaching. But canine use of vocalizations is minimal, compared to ours, given the vast amount of communicating that they typically do in a day. It was featured in the movie not because dogs actually communicate that way, but because humans place such a high value on verbal communication that many of us can't imagine doing it any other way.

If I were to visit Italy or Greece, for example, I would be lost because I don't have the skills for adequate verbal communication with people there. But if I sent my dog to Italy or Greece, my dog would be able to communicate just fine with every dog that lives there. That's because dogs are fluent in body language, which is universal. I can go to any country in the world, and communicate with the dogs there very well, and they can communicate with me. The body language we use is identical in all of those places.

Body Language

Dogs understand all your subtle cues of body language, including the cues that identify you to them as a leader. And it doesn't matter where the animals come from. My husband, Jason, had an experience in Baghdad which illustrates that. Jason was in the Iraqi capital on a security assignment, and he and several men he worked with came upon a pack of about 10 stray dogs.

The dogs approached Jason and the other men to see if they could obtain food and, because of his dog-training background, Jason could clearly see the rank structure within the pack. He was closely watching the behavior of the animals, and he could see which dog was in charge of the others. Another pack member that stood out from the rest was an old dog which, because of his age, didn't have the strength or the stamina of most of the younger ones. As a result, the one in command bullied the old dog quite a bit.

Jason took a liking to the old dog, but as the pack approached, the pack leader did not allow the old one to enter Jason's proximity, a six-foot area that trainers call the "domineering zone." This offended Jason a bit, so he corrected the pack leader; not with words, but with body language that included eye contact and some low-key hand signals. Jason prohibited the leader from coming within his six-foot zone, but befriended the old dog by allowing it into his inner circle.

It's hard to describe precisely what all of Jason's physical actions were, because they were so subtle. Perhaps the example of a police officer on duty will illustrate what I'm talking about. A police officer needs to take immediate control of any out-of-the-ordinary situation he or she encounters on patrol. The officer normally does so primarily by employing body language. This involves an array of things that include posture, eye contact, proximity to others, the appearance of confidence and possibly additional signals that an officer broadcasts. Taken together, they send the message, "I am in charge here, and you will defer to me." Most of the time, the officer doesn't even have to raise his voice.

Canines have the rare ability to pick up on the subtlest of cues. Often they are cues that you may not have intended to send. Here's an illustration of how that can work. When I enter my training and boarding facility I'm usually wearing a T-shirt and jeans and comfortable athletic shoes. I move with confidence. I feel like I'm in charge of the place, I look like I'm in charge of the place, and as far as the dogs are concerned I am in charge of the place, because that's the image that I project. Occasionally, however, when I still lived on the property, I would enter the building at night in a fuzzy bathrobe and high-heeled slippers. As I moved about the building to carry out whatever errand brought me there, clutching the robe to keep it closed and trying to balance on the heels, it was obvious that the dogs didn't accord me the same deference that they normally did. That's because of what I call the "injured-bird syndrome." With my mincing steps and balancing issues, I projected vulnerability.

Jason, in the Baghdad incident, projected the opposite of vulnerability. Rather than an injured bird, he was the police officer in the midst of a situation. The dogs were attentive to his cues, and deferred to his wishes.

Jason's companions were amazed as they watched this play out. Even though they were hungry, the dogs were more interested in Jason than they were in his companions, some of whom carried corn chips, because Jason offered meaningful interaction that they were programmed to understand.

The fact is Jason used the same communication techniques the dogs would use within the pack. None of it involved verbal language.

Dogs can learn the simple meanings of many words, and we do want to teach them to respond to verbal commands. But as humans, we tend to place too much emphasis on it.

I have imported several dogs into the United States from Europe, and of course the dogs that get off an airplane at our international airport have been raised in the environment of a different human language than the one they encounter here. That's highly irrelevant to them, however, about the time I clip my leash to their collar. They understand my intentions as a result of the power of that line, through which I transmit signals to them about what they and I are going to do.

Many of the dogs that I have imported had been exposed only to one language – German. They certainly would respond to German commands with which they were familiar. But more important to them was body language. Meeting a new dog that had been raised primarily with another language never has been an obstacle for me, because when I meet him he speaks not German, but dog. When he starts to communicate with me, I know exactly what he's saying.

I'm discussing this not because you are likely to import a dog that has been raised in an environment other than English, but to emphasize that spoken language – *any* spoken language – is significantly less important to a dog than body language.

You can make this aspect of a dog's nature work for you. Through training, you can learn how to be a strong and confident leader and how to project those qualities and other communications through body language. A dog feels comfortable with that.

Dogs learn canine body language from their mothers and litter mates. When dogs integrate into our human world, they start to learn human body language as well, through observation. A lot of similarities exist between human and canine body language, and also many differences. The differences can be important. Some of the differences are responsible for why dogs bite so many children around the face.

Small children, for example, following their instincts for human body language, view hugging a dog around its neck as a loving gesture. The dog, however, may very likely see that act from a stranger as a threat, or the same act from a subordinate as a sign of disrespect. They are likely to correct that *faux pas* with a nip to the face or head, just as they would when dealing with a canine in an identical situation.

Children also tend to be very direct in their approach, and often will move straight in on a dog they don't know. A dog, on the other hand, expects an unfamiliar entity to approach more cautiously. A dominant dog that sees a child approach at Mach 2 speed may well view it as a disrespectful move, and may correct that individual for showing disrespect. A dog that lacks confidence could view it as a threat, and might bite in self-defense.

Because of these inborn differences, dogs must be socialized at a critical age to the presence of children. We deal a lot with this issue with our clients' dogs. Differences between the body language of people and dogs do exist. However, dogs can learn by continued exposure and by observation to reinterpret human body language and to recognize when it is or is not a threat.

The Senses

In our culture, people and dogs have become so integrated in each other's lives, and people often hold dogs in such high regard, that many of us feature dogs prominently in our family portraits. The likenesses of our dogs often find a place in personalized family holiday cards, as well, and we know that some families celebrate their dogs' birthdays in a fashion similar to the way they celebrate the birthdays of children.

Despite all of the integration and affection, however, significant differences exist between canines and people, and they bear thinking about. The human brain is dominated by a large visual cortex, for example. A dog's brain is dominated by a large olfactory cortex, which relates to the sense of smell. A dog's general visual acuity is poor compared to a human's. Scientists believe that what a dog sees is like a slightly out-of-focus photograph, a little fuzzy and rough around the edges. They think that dogs have an especially hard time seeing in poor light, which under some circumstances may induce anxiety and stress in a dog. In a normal dog, this problem usually results at least in a heightened state of alertness in low-light situations, and can influence the kinds of decisions the dog makes in response to what it sees, or what it thinks it sees.

A dog's hearing, on the other hand, tends to be significantly sharper than a human's. A dog not only can hear things that are pitched too high for a human to hear at all, but can hear most things better than a human even within the frequency range that's audible to the human ear. And he can pinpoint the location of a sound with great accuracy.

A dog often can hear a vehicle pulling into the driveway, for example, when the humans of the household are unable to detect it. Not only that, he can tell whether that vehicle is Dad's pickup truck, Grandma's Volkswagen bug or a car he's unfamiliar with. At our training and boarding facility, we usually place a dog in one of our outside runs sometime before his owner is scheduled to arrive to retrieve him, and we can tell by his behavior when the owner is about to appear. Judging by the time that elapses, we have discovered that many of our dogs detect their owner's vehicle when it is still a quarter-mile or more from our facility, and they show excitement only for their owner's vehicle and not for any others. Some of them, in fact, are able to

distinguish between vehicles of the same make and model, acknowledging the pending arrival of their owner and ignoring the pending arrival of someone else in a similar vehicle.

Of all the senses, however, the sense of smell is the most important one to most dogs. A dog's ability to smell is millions of times more sensitive than a person's. It is their most reliable sense, and the one they use to confirm and validate information that they gather through the other senses, the way that humans use vision to confirm their other senses. This is a fundamental and very important difference between people and dogs.

Imagine this scenario, and you'll understand how it works: A human is on the witness stand in court, and a defense attorney is questioning him.

"How do you know that the subject returned to the house that night?" the defense attorney asks.

"Because I heard him come in," the witness replies.

"Yes," the attorney might say, "but did you actually *see* him?"

Now pretend that a dog is on the witness stand in a canine court of law. The same scenario is occurring.

"How do you know that the subject returned to the house that night?" the doggy defense attorney asks.

"Because I heard him come in," the witness replies.

"Yes," the lawyer would say, "but did you actually *smell* him?"

Smell, not sight, provides the ultimate evidence to the canine brain.

Let me tell you how this phenomenon works in real life. Years ago, when I was attending a school for professional dog trainers on the East Coast, I and other students at the school trained in man-trailing with bloodhounds. Every day at 6 a.m., we followed a scent trail in the Appalachian Mountains, and after several months of training, we students thought we were pretty good at it. Finally, our instructors administered a test. They divided us into several teams. Each team was assigned an experienced bloodhound. And for each team, an instructor went out and laid down a nearly identical two-hour trail. Then they turned us loose to see which of our teams could find the instructor and which of us could do it the fastest.

Bloodhounds are amazing animals. Like many other hound breeds, they track primarily by following a scent trail laid down on the ground, rather than by pulling the scent out of the air. And, like other hound breeds, their ability to smell is so incredibly sensitive that they can strike a trail and determine in just moments the direction their quarry is traveling. They apparently do it by analyzing the infinitesimal differences in the strength of the scent along the track. In the direction of the quarry's travel, the scent becomes minutely stronger. In the direction from which the quarry came, the scent grows weaker. That's how we think it works, anyway, although hounds have yet to share with us how they actually accomplish this remarkable feat. All hounds track in a similar way, and all are adept at determining direction of travel.

Over the weeks of our bloodhound training, our instructors tried to foster in us respect for our dogs' abilities, and to drill into us the importance of trusting them. Our canine partners are experts, the instructors explained, and we should pay attention to what they tell us through their actions.

So, there we were, out in the hills on test day with our hound, running a trail that had been laid down some time before and that was invisible to us. An hour or more into the trail, it led along the edge of a muddy cow pasture. My team followed the scent, our bloodhound in the lead at the end of a 30-foot leash. All of a sudden, we came to a spot where our instructor had turned sharply and struck out across the pasture. It was perfectly obvious to us, because we could see his tracks – plain as day – leaving the solid ground at the edge of the pasture and going out through the mud.

When we reached the spot, our dog showed some momentary confusion.

He cast about for a moment, and then decided to ignore the tracks in the mud and to set out in a different direction. The dog could see the tracks just as we could, but the sight of them did not constitute significant evidence for him. He wanted to go a different way.

For us, it was perfectly obvious the dog was making a mistake. We could see the tracks with our own eyes, after all. And so we pulled him off the trail that he wanted to follow, and insisted that he follow the tracks across the pasture. Eventually, the tracks in the mud disappeared as the ground became harder, and our dog showed greater and greater confusion. Impatient with the hound's "incompetence," we students insisted that he continue to search in the direction the tracks last headed.

To make a long story short, our team lost the competition. Our instructor had set a trap for us. He had doubled back out of the pasture and had continued along the original route that he was on before entering the mud. He didn't fool the dog. Our dog knew what the instructor had done, because his nose told him. But we humans had overruled the dog because we thought the evidence we had gathered with our eyes was more dependable than the evidence he had gathered with his nose.

It was not.

This was a learning moment for all of us on that team, and I never forgot it.

So, how do people learn? People learn in many ways, and in this case I learned by making a mistake.

How Dogs Learn

Dogs learn the same way – by making a mistake. Dogs also learn through repetition, which is their primary path to new skills. And they also learn by watching people or other dogs. I will talk about these learning techniques in detail in subsequent chapters.

Here's something to keep in mind, however. While many dogs will look to their owner or handler for information or for solutions to a problem, most normal dogs will always look to another dog first if another dog is available. This will have a profound effect on training dogs in a multi-dog household. Your new dog will look to your adult resident dog first for learning rules of the house and for solutions to problems that it encounters. The resident dog can be a great help in this regard. Or, it can be a great hindrance, because it will teach a new dog all of its own good habits and all of its bad ones.

Let me tell you a true story that shows how this can work. We have a client at our training facility who owned a mid-sized dog that was genetically unsound, which meant it was psychologically unstable. Her family loved the dog, but it had a lot of behavior problems because it was not wired correctly. She called on us for help with the dog, and we were able to assist significantly with some of the behavioral issues. But, of course, we could not correct the underlying genetic problem.

The family decided they wanted a second dog in their household, and I counseled them about what to expect. The new dog would look to the resident dog for information, I explained, and so they needed to intervene in the new puppy's upbringing as much as possible.

Unfortunately, our client did not do so to the extent required, and the adult resident dog essentially reared the puppy. The puppy was a genetically sound animal, but the resident dog raised him to be a 110-pound adult that was nervous and unsure of himself, and taught him to bring aggression to the table when under stress. The family eventually decided that this young dog had become too dangerous to keep and, with heavy hearts, had him euthanized.

Less than six months later they decided to get another genetically sound new puppy. We urged them to be much more instrumental in the puppy's upbringing this time and, again, they were not. About two years later they had the second dog euthanized, for the same reasons.

Chapter 3

Choosing Your Companion Dog

Whoever said you can't buy happiness forgot little puppies.

– Gene Hill

The most important thing you can do in choosing a dog of any age is to check your emotions at the door. It sounds hard-hearted, I know, but human emotions can wreak havoc on a good plan. You need to walk into an acquisition situation with your eyes and ears wide open, your emotions in check, and your brain primed to make a sound decision.

This is especially essential when you're dealing with puppies. There isn't a puppy that you're not going to fall in love with, because they're all adorable. But a cool head can be important with dogs of any age. Let me share with you the experience of a close personal friend of mine.

She wanted a companion for her medium-sized dog of a popular breed. She had a male, and I urged her to shop for a female, to complement him. So she went on the Internet, looking all over the state for a female of the same breed. Finally she found one on the opposite side of the state, and began an e-mail correspondence with the dog's owner.

I had warned her to check her emotions at the door. She had planned to do that, but she never had encountered anyone like the owner of this dog, who turned out to be a master of psychology. The owner sent her pictures of this beautiful dog, along with e-mail letters in the dog's voice that said things such as, "I like long walks on the beach, snuggling in bed and tummy rubs."

My friend was just blown away.

"I'm getting this dog," she told me.

"You haven't even met this dog," I replied.

"I know, but I've fallen in love with her. We've been writing back and forth."

"The *dog* has been writing back and forth?" I asked. "Don't you mean its owner has been writing?"

"Well, yes, but it's like the dog has been writing, and I know her enough, and I love her already," my friend explained.

Wow! Walks on the beach and sipping margaritas in the rain, and my friend is in love! She purchased the dog.

Fortunately, her story has a happy ending. The new dog turned out not to be everything she expected, and they had a bumpy ride to start, but my friend stuck with it and things worked out all right in the end.

Breeds and Breed Types

The mistake my friend made was not that unusual. A lot of people render decisions based on emotion rather than facts. But since you will be making a 14-year commitment to this animal, give or take, it's best if your decision is based on the most factual information you can get.

Is that cocker spaniel really the cute little rascal he appears to be? Will that Alaskan malamute blend in readily with your young urban family? Will that jolly old black Lab be as playful all the time as he seems to be on first meeting? How do you find a dog that's best suited to your lifestyle?

For generations, people have sought a companion from within a breed or a breed type that produces animals with characteristics they consider desirable.

A breed is a collection of animals descended from common ancestors, usually through selective breeding, and that displays similar attributes and characteristics and meets certain common standards, either physical or behavioral or both. Official breeds usually are recognized by a governing or administrative body, such as the American Kennel Club. A breed *type* is an animal descended from a mixture of breeds, and displays a mixture of characteristics, but often one breed's characteristics predominate. The breed whose characteristics predominate would be the dog's "breed type."

Here's something to keep in mind, however. Obtaining a dog of a particular breed, even though it may be a purebred dog with official "papers," does not necessarily mean that it will accurately reflect every descriptive phrase the American Kennel Club uses to extol its breed. In fact, greater individual differences often exist within a group, such as a breed, than exist on average between some groups.

Look at differences, for example, that exist between two major groups of humans we're all familiar with –women and men. We can say with statistical certainty that men generally are larger than women. Men tend to be physically stronger than women. Men also tend to be less nurturing than women, and usually don't live as long as women. All of those statements are correct, as

A German shepherd dog cross (left) whose breed type obviously is German shepherd dog.

A "goldendoodle," (below) the product of a golden retriever and French poodle cross. Judging by appearance, breed type probably is French poodle.

they apply to the two large categories of people. However, we all know that some women are larger than some men. We know that some women athletes are stronger than all but the strongest men. Many of us know men who are as nurturing as any woman and, conversely, women who are not nurturing at all, and we all know of women who fail to outlive their mates.

My point is that breed characteristics serve only as the most general guide. They're a good starting point in a search, but within every breed you will find a wide range of variables, and you need to focus your search carefully on individuals.

You can find breed information from books, from on-line sources, from professional breeders, from veterinarians and from professional trainers and canine behaviorists. A word of caution, though: Very often the information derived from organizations that publish it or post it on-line lists only the most sterling qualities for each of the breeds. Such descriptions might include great love of children, undying fidelity toward family, super intelligence and so forth. They tend to gloss over less endearing but equally noteworthy qualities in some cases such as, for example, possible aggressive tendencies, stubbornness, aversion to children and things such as that.

You need to approach breeders with a similar sense of caution. On the plus side, they're usually quite knowledgeable about the breed with which they work. The downside is that this particular breed often is their favorite, which is why they work with it, and they may not be the best source to go to for unbiased information when you're weighing one breed against another.

A more neutral source of information may be a veterinarian, a trainer or a behaviorist. These are people who usually work with many breeds under many different circumstances and levels of stress, and they usually are in a good position to assess both high points and low points of all of them. Keep in mind, though, that many veterinarians focus primarily on physical issues with their patients and less so on behavioral ones.

It's important to understand something about canine characteristics and personality types: Personalities do vary among individuals of the same canine breed, sometimes to a remarkable degree. Nevertheless, members of the same breed tend to share broad behavioral characteristics in common; that is in fact the reason the various breeds were developed. Members of some breeds like to hunt or to track, some like to retrieve, some to herd, some to protect people or animals for which they're responsible, and so forth. So if you're looking for a purebred dog, you really want to do your research on the breeds. The rule of

Black and tan coonhound, a type of dog whose life revolves around its olfactory system.

thumb with a rescue dog is that the breed of dog the canine most resembles has provided the dominant genes that he's carrying in his makeup. Sometimes we'll find a surprise or two in the package, but over the years I've found this to be a useful way of predicting broad outlines of personality and behavior in mixed-breed dogs. If your dog looks predominantly Rottweiler, expect its behavior to be predominantly Rottweiler as well. If your dog looks predominantly cocker spaniel, expect its behavior to be, also.

Aside from four feet and – usually – a tail, what do most dogs have in common? Not necessarily a heck of a lot. Under their doggy exteriors, canines are no more likely to be identical in personality than are people. In some respects, that's one of the most fascinating things about dogs. They come in nearly infinite varieties, just like people, and this gives us an opportunity to find a unique companion who really will hit it off with us.

Often, people will see a dog that is visually appealing, perhaps in a book or a magazine or on the street, and will decide that that's the kind of dog they want. Sometimes they do this without knowing anything about breed temper-

Mini Australian shepherds, a high-energy breed despite their relatively small size.

ament or breed characteristics, and that's a mistake.

You probably exercise a lot of care in choosing your friends, and you owe it to yourself to use the same degree of care in choosing a canine companion. Sometimes it can be hit-or-miss, but the more effort and thought you put into it, the greater the likelihood that you'll be pleased with the result.

By the way, in talking about breed characteristics, I am not implying that only purebred dogs make worthy companions. Rescue dogs can make an excellent addition to your household. But the point is we need to analyze our own lifestyle and choose a dog that will embrace it, or at least adapt to it. Are you a single guy who runs marathons? Would you like a high-energy dog to accompany you on training runs? You probably don't want an English bulldog or an English bulldog cross. If you're a woman in your 80s, you might not want a high-energy dog like a terrier or a pointing dog. You might prefer one whose idea of a great time is lying on your lap while you read novellas.

Do you have a family with a lot of small children? Is the dog you're considering one that will enjoy a busy household with a lot of noise and confusion?

Do you live alone in a tiny studio apartment on the 26th floor of your building? Is the dog you're considering one that's content to lie all day in blissful contemplation while you're gone, or one that yearns for a large herd of cattle or sheep to drive from the lower 40 to the upper 40 and then back again?

Energy level isn't the only thing to consider when thinking about acquiring a dog, however. Another thing to consider is climate. Try to choose a breed or a breed type that's suited to the weather where you live. At our boarding facility, we have a climate-controlled building that we keep at a comfortable 62 degrees year-round. Most dogs love it. But Siberian huskies and Alaskan malamutes protest if they have to go into the building in the winter. They find it too warm. They want to be outside.

By the same token, our Mexican Chihuahua would not like to move to Fairbanks, Alaska. She's running a little chilly, in fact, right here in Western Washington. But she would do great in Phoenix. If our German shepherd dog had to move to Fairbanks, he wouldn't mind at all.

An English bulldog with a delightful personality. But his short legs and inefficient cooling system preclude him from marathon running.

Does Size Matter?

Another thing to consider is a dog's size. Obviously if you live in that studio apartment on the 26th floor, you probably aren't looking for a Great Dane, a Saint Bernard or even a Chesapeake Bay retriever. Let the guy with 40 acres of meadows and his own private pond provide a home for animals like those. But here's something to be aware of: Just because a dog is small doesn't mean it will fit contentedly into a small space. This takes us back to breed characteristics.

Let me tell you about an older gentleman who walked into our training center one day with a 10-month old terrier. She was a member of a small breed of terrier, and she was exhibiting severe behavioral problems. She'd spin in circles for what seemed like hours, this fellow said, would pace back and forth almost constantly, and would lick the inside of the sliding glass kitchen door until it seemed as if her tongue must bleed. When he let her out into the fenced back yard, she would dig and dig and dig. He wanted these behaviors to stop.

We assessed this dog, and discovered that she was a sweet little pup. However, we determined that her behaviors arose from frustration, boredom and anxiety that resulted from her experiencing little active engagement with her owner. We discovered through conversation with him that he had little meaningful interaction with the dog except to let her in and out of the sliding glass door to the yard.

Being a terrier, this was a high-energy dog in spite of her small size. She needed long walks and play time and opportunity to run. We laid out a doggy exercise regimen for the man that would begin with him snapping on her leash several times a day to take her for walks outside the back yard so she could burn energy and engage her inquisitive mind in things of interest outside her yard.

He told us that he didn't do leashes, and didn't do walks.

"Well, okay," I replied. "Do you happen to have an exercise treadmill at home?"

He said he did.

"I can train your dog to use the treadmill," I told him. All you have to do is leash her up and put her on it, and it will be a great way for her to burn off excess energy."

"I told you," the owner responded, "I don't do leashes."

His idea of a perfect day would be to relax in his recliner, his little dog in his lap, and to scratch her ears while they watched TV together. He had brought his beautiful little animal to us for a "cure," and apparently had hoped that we could turn his 10-month-old terrier into a 12-year-old basset hound.

There isn't a trainer on the planet who can do that, and so we returned the man's money and watched him walk out the door with his dog. It broke our hearts to see her go. She was such a sweetheart of a pup, and all she wanted out of life was what virtually any terrier would want: exercise and engagement. Unfortunately, the man most certainly had not chosen wisely in selecting the kind of dog to fit his lifestyle, and sadly, the primary victim of his mistake was the dog.

Gender

Which gender is better in a companion dog? Neither is better – or worse – in every situation.

Male and female dogs both are great, for different reasons. It's like comparing an apple and an onion. Both can be great family dogs. Both can be great with children, and even with small children. Subtle differences do tend to show up between the genders, however, and depending on what breed we're talking about, these differences can become significant. As a very loose guideline, females tend to be more nurturing of small children. This could be beneficial to you or it could be not so beneficial.

For example, some of my female German shepherd dogs, which are herding dogs, tend to have strong maternal instincts, which can be a nice combination with children. However, as a visitor I would not want to get in the way of a female German shepherd dog or a female Rottweiler that was tending to the small children in her house. She would be a force to be reckoned with. A female German shepherd dog is likely to protect her human babies as intently as she would protect her own puppies. And this could be a problem when your neighbor suddenly pops in to borrow a cup of sugar.

While females generally tend to behave in a more nurturing manner, by the way, there are many exceptions to the rule. I've seen many males that exhibit highly nurturing behavior also.

Compatibility

Another thing you want to take into consideration: Suppose you are getting a second dog as a companion for an existing dog. It is important that you get a type of dog that complements the type you already have. This applies not only to breed, but to gender and to age.

Let me tell you a story about how things can go wrong. We had some really good clients who had a delightful old redbone hound who was edging into his golden years. Redbones are large and solid, stable and dependable dogs bred to trail game such as bears, cougars and raccoons. Generally, not much can fluster them, and my clients' dog not only exhibited all of the common breed characteristics, but he was approaching a time of life when he wanted to settle into a sort of retirement.

My clients wanted him to have a nice companion, so they decided to go with a rescue dog, and chose a female – which was a good idea to balance the fact that the old redbone was male. Sometimes, two males or two females in the same house will not bring harmony. Disharmony doesn't always result, but the possibility is worth considering.

So far, so good. But here, the decision-making fell apart. The people selected a very young female, and it wasn't a redbone. In fact, it wasn't any sort of hound breed at all. It was a pit bull. The pit bull really was a sweetie, but she was a high-energy dog who hit their house like a hurricane. If you think of the redbone as an elderly gent sipping a small glass of mellow wine, the pit bull was a Roller Derby queen tossing back triple-shot espressos. The dogs couldn't have been more different. The redbone lived life in the slow lane, the pit bull in the hammer lane.

This was a match made in a nightmare. The dogs were wired differently. They perceived things differently. They functioned differently.

The result was lots of quarrels and a loss of harmony in the home. Finally, the owners decided in the interest of peace to maintain the dogs separately. The dogs' lives came to revolve around different baby gates, living in different rooms, eating separately and enjoying different walk times.

To the owners' credit, they refused to give up on the pit bull. As far as they were concerned, she was not a throw-away dog. Once they had made a commitment to her they were determined to see it through, and they did. Theirs was a very noble position.

But if they had used more care in picking the companion, they could have enjoyed a significantly different four or five years between the time the new dog came into their home and the time the old dog passed away.

Here's another example of how compatibility tends to work among dogs. During major holiday periods, our boarding facilities at Camano Island Kennels usually are completely booked. Such was the case around one recent holiday. Our guests included several members of the hound group, several members of the retriever group, a number of dogs that functioned similarly to retrievers, and several members of toy breeds, as well as other miscellaneous breeds and breed types.

During this particular holiday week our visitors included a bloodhound, a redbone, a basset hound and two beagles. We put them all in proximity to one another, in the same section of the building, which became for that week the hound section of our building.

We also had some Labrador retrievers, some golden retrievers and a couple of Dalmatians, which are not retrievers but which function like retrievers. We grouped them in what became the retriever section of the building.

In yet another section we grouped members of several toy breeds.

We knew that a six-pound Maltese might not care to be bunked next door to a 100-pound Rottweiler. Most of the various breeds at our facility that holiday week were grouped with other breeds that function similarly, and they did quite well boarding in proximity to one another. It brought harmony to them and to our facility.

Often, when we put groups of dogs outdoors to exercise and to socialize, we put them out in groups like this as well.

All of the factors we've discussed here are things you should give thoughtful attention to in choosing your canine companion; breed or breed type, size, gender and energy level, as well as compatibility issues if you already have a dog in your home. Another factor also is of major significance in selecting your dog, and that is a particular dog's temperament. In fact, this issue can be of such great importance that I have devoted much of the next chapter to discussing it.

Chapter 4

Canine Temperament

Dogs have more good in them than men think they have.

– Chinese proverb

Temperament is a tricky thing to assess in a dog or in any other animal, including humans. But it can be critically important.

Temperament encompasses characteristics of canine personality such as friendliness, shyness, aggressiveness, protectiveness and responsiveness to training. A canine's temperament type appears to be determined genetically at the time of conception, although many researchers think it can be modified later at least to some extent by environment.

In some cases, however, a dog's temperament may be judged to be "unsound," and that cannot be corrected.

The fact that unsoundness is not correctible has led to unfortunate results for a lot of dogs. Over the years, I've seen many dogs euthanized in shelters, in rescue situations and by private owners because someone made an assessment that the dog was "crazy." More often than not, the dog was not unsound, in my opinion, and the person who made the assessment was wrong. I haven't conducted a survey, but I believe, based on my years of experience, that the number of unsound dogs walking the planet is very, very low. Unfortunately, thousands of dogs – if not millions – are euthanized unnecessarily every year, not because they are genetically unsound, which is a permanent condition, but because of bad behavior, which usually can be corrected.

A dog that is unsound is one that cannot process information correctly. This results in social problems with people and with other canines, and can be manifested in behaviors that range all the way from overt and inappropriate submissiveness to uncontrolled aggression.

Although we can't fix unsoundness, sometimes we can modify the behavior of an unsound dog enough so that we can live with it.

Remember this, however. A dog is either sound or unsound. There is no middle ground. A dog can be sound and still have behavioral issues. But when it is unsound, its wiring and default settings are not correct, and no amount of training can fix them. The dog always will be abnormal.

A similar concept applies to people. I can think of a couple of modern-day American criminals who obviously were unsound people. But, because they were human beings and had the ability to think rationally – at least some of the time – they were able to hide their true character from many people for years. Dogs, on the other hand, do not have this ability. They will show us through their behavior everything there is to know about them if we watch closely enough. An experienced person usually can detect canine unsoundness fairly easily, especially if the dog is removed from its normal surroundings. In the security of its home, and in the presence of its owner, some of its behavior can be masked. But when the dog is removed from this environment, the behaviors usually will make themselves clear.

It's a good idea, therefore, to try to get a reading on the soundness and the temperament of any dog you are considering for acquisition, and it helps to have specialized knowledge and expertise in doing so. Some people use a written checklist and a series of tests to do a temperament evaluation, and some just observe the animal, but all are looking essentially for the same things. A layman with a checklist can learn a lot of things about a dog, but the process would not be as productive as it would if it were done by a person with experience in conducting this evaluation.

Here's something worth considering, however. I have found that evidence of unsoundness usually is easiest to detect on the day a dog arrives at a shelter or other receiving facility. The dog usually is experiencing relatively high stress then as a result of being in a new and possibly strange environment, and its insecurities tend to magnify the evidence of unsound condition.

At many shelters, on the other hand, temperament assessments often are deliberately postponed for at least 72 hours, until after a dog has had a chance to adjust somewhat to its new environment and its stress level has gone down. This is because shelter staffs generally are not trying to detect unsoundness, per se, but rather are looking at a dog's array of normal temperament characteristics in order to match the dog better with a new home. Staff members know that those characteristics can be disguised by the stress that's often present on intake day. A normally outgoing dog may be shy and subdued, for example, or a naturally aggressive dog may not reveal its aggressive tendencies until after it feels more at home in the new environment.

If you are presented with an intake assessment or temperament analysis, it is helpful to know when it was done.

Another important thing to keep in mind: While some unsound dogs are dangerous, not all are. We had a dog in one of our basic obedience classes recently, for example, that exhibited some classic unsound behavior. The day was rainy, and we decided to train indoors at our facility, in our upstairs training hall. This dog went up the stairs with his owner and nine or 10 other dogs and their owners, but when he got to the second floor he went into a panicked crawl. The floor there is of textured wood that is not slippery to a dog's feet, and most dogs like it. Because of its texture, however, it creates a somewhat unusual sound under a dog's toenails. A padded mat covers most of the floor, but a stretch of bare, textured wood remains between the door and the mat.

All of the dogs in the class but one came up the stairs and walked or trotted across the textured floor to the mat with no problem. But dog number ten hit the ground with his belly as soon as his feet touched the floor, and crawled from the door to the mat. As soon as he reached the mat, he regained his feet and walked just fine. But as the hour-long lesson went on, he became increasingly phobic about the textured floor. He went out of his way to avoid touching it, and if he did touch it, he immediately pressed his belly to the ground as though he were afraid he was about to fall off the edge of the earth.

The significant thing is not that he was afraid of the floor, but that he took his fear to a phobic level. The point is – and this is the key – that he was unable to recover psychologically from his initial scare. It is normal for dogs to be startled from time to time. The wind blows over a garbage can, perhaps, and a dog jumps in reaction. But once he sees that the noise is not a threat, just a garbage can rolling in the wind, we expect him to begin to recover and go about his business. Webster's New World Dictionary defines phobia as an irrational, excessive and persistent fear of a thing or situation. "Irrational" and "excessive" are the key words here. In the case of the dog in our class, no amount of training will overcome his problems. The significant thing is not that the floor triggered a negative response, but that the response was phobic. If a textured floor doesn't upset him, something else will.

Adult Dogs

If you're planning to buy or adopt an adult dog, it's best to obtain a dependable evaluation of your future companion's temperament. It's hard to do one correctly yourself if you're not a professional. But if you see any behavior that strikes you as aggressive, especially if you have children at home, you've found a potential red flag. Remember, so many thousands of dogs need homes, that if you don't find one today you might find one in the same place tomorrow or next week. So don't be in a hurry. Decline to take any dog that exhibits behavior that raises your eyebrow.

The people who work at your dog's kennel or shelter may or may not be doing their own evaluations, and they may or may not be doing them correctly. In any case, while such evaluations can be helpful, I wouldn't necessarily place myself solely in their hands. You can hire your own expert if you wish, and it might be a good investment, depending on your resources. You're not looking just for a trainer, however, but for a behaviorist. Although many professional trainers have enough experience to do the job, many do not. You can search for a canine behaviorist on-line, or ask veterinarians for a referral. When you find a behaviorist, check his credentials, and ask whether he can provide testimonials from clients.

Also, ask the organization from which you are buying or adopting about its return policy. Suppose you take a dog home and some behaviors begin to show after a week or two that indicate the dog is not suitable for your family?

Puppies

It's equally important to do a temperament assessment if you're buying a pup, and they often are easier to do with pups than with adult dogs. If possible, evaluate the whole litter or a majority of the whole litter together and, if possible, evaluate the pups' parents, as well.

What is the best way to pick a puppy? When I go to see a litter of pups, I usually insist on meeting the mother. It's not a bad idea to take a look at the father, as well, if he is on site, because he and the mother contribute equally to the genetic makeup of the pups. Often the father is located elsewhere, however, so seeing him is not possible. But that's okay, because the mother is more important, and here's why: While both parents contribute equally to their offsprings' DNA, it's the mother that actually raises the pups for the first two months or more of their lives. A puppy's brain is fully developed by seven weeks of age, and it is the mother that is critical in laying a strong foundation for the pup in terms of behavioral characteristics it will possess or not possess for the rest of its life.

A sound, stable mother as a teacher usually will pass on to you a sound, stable pup. But if you have an unsound, unstable mother as the teacher, you will have a litter full of unstable, emotionally unsettled puppies, and you may never be able to correct it completely. Human intervention rarely can undo her influence if it has been negative for the first seven or eight weeks of the puppies' lives.

The thing that you primarily do not want to see in the mother is timidity and fearfulness. She will have taught her pups, by her own example, to behave the same way.

It is better to see the mother out of the presence of her puppies. That way, she does not have to be concerned about protecting them from you, a stranger, although she still may be a bit leery about the presence of a stranger on the property. So cut her a little slack for that.

You are looking for a dog that is confident, interested and willing to engage with you or to investigate you. I like to see a dog that's inquisitive, but if she's not inquisitive about me I won't force myself on her. She doesn't have to be my best friend. But the biggest problem is if she's fearful or shy. An even bigger red flag is if she is fearful and shy to the point of aggression.

So you've met the mother, and she passes muster, and now you have a dynamic litter of pups before you, a variety of temperaments. How do you go about choosing? The choice you make depends on the kind of dog you are seeking. Will this be a hunting dog? A herding dog? A police-service or personal-protection dog? Or will it be a companion dog?

I prefer to see an entire litter of pups together, or at least as many of them as are on site, even if not all of them are available for sale to me. That way, I can observe the widest possible range of interactions.

If I am looking for a companion dog, I will be looking for a pup that falls into the middle of the personality range. I won't want the shyest puppy in the pack, nor the most outgoing. The most inquisitive puppy in the litter very possibly is a future leadership entity. Depending on what type of entity I am, I may not want a dog that believes he's a leader. I may be significantly more comfortable with a dog that enjoys the role of follower. On the other hand, I don't want a shy or fearful dog.

If you don't have professional help, evaluate the pups to the best of your ability. Take note of behaviors that appear to be normal. If things that seem a little peculiar catch your eye, pay attention to them. Suppose that while you're watching the litter of pups, you see one that appears to be the alpha. Is he a bully? Is behavior that's cute at seven or eight weeks of age going to be cute as the animal grows older? Perhaps the behavior of the pup you're watching is not so unusual as to indicate unsoundness, but maybe you don't want a very strong entity as your companion dog. Maybe you do, but if you don't, pay attention to this.

Perhaps one of the pups in the litter is antisocial, not interested in interacting with people or in a playful way with his littermates. That should raise an eyebrow. What many professional observers look for is a pup whose social behavior ranges somewhere in the middle of the scale; not at either extreme.

If it's not nap time, 20 or 30 minutes are going to tell me what I need to know as long as I'm paying attention, and it won't make any difference whether the owner is with me or not. I would prefer to observe the pups away from their mom and in a new environment, either indoors or outdoors, not in an environment they've already explored for hours or for days, so I can see who is willing to investigate new things and to engage, and who is not willing.

I like a pup that is at least eight weeks of age. I want him to have had his mother's influence for the full eight weeks, because it is she that is going to teach him how to be a dog. If he has not had that opportunity with her it's a red flag for me.

I know that a pup's critical socialization window closes at 16 weeks so, while eight weeks is preferable, I want him to be no older than 10 or 11 weeks of age when I obtain him, because I've got a lot of work to get done with him by the time he reaches 16 weeks. I'll explore the subject of socialization more completely in Chapter 8.

Rescue Dogs

Are you thinking about adopting a dog that you believe needs to be rescued from neglect or abuse?

It's a commendable thing to do, and many people find top-notch canine companions that way. With more than 75 million dogs in the United States, a lot of them need to be rescued, and you often can find a previously neglected or abused canine at your local animal shelter or dog-adoption agency.

But here are a couple of things to think about before you make that leap. First, many of the dogs you find at animal shelters are not really rescue dogs at all. A lot of them simply are "previously owned," so you may want to look into the background of your dog if carrying out a rescue really is important to you. Second, even if the dog you find at a shelter is a legitimate rescue dog – one that has been neglected or physically or emotionally abused – chances are that by the time you meet the animal its rescue already has been accomplished. The rescue is completed just as soon as the dog is out of harm's way, and that's usually about the time it goes into the shelter or the adoption agency. Some adoptive owners, being good-hearted people, take the animal home and continue to "rescue" it long after its neglect or abuse, if any, has ceased, sometimes for years after. Not only does this not help the dog, it actually may harm it.

Also, think about this: While you may find a wonderful canine companion at an animal shelter or adoption agency, it's also possible to return home with an animal that has problems of such magnitude that they are uncorrectable. So, it's wise to proceed with caution and not to let your heart overrule your head.

A dog may have serious problems as a result of its life experiences or it may have them because of its *lack* of life experiences. A lot of newer pet owners assume that their dog's problems, if any, result from horrible things that have happened to it. More often, however, problems result from things that have *not* happened, such as socialization and training.

How can you tell if the animal you are considering truly is a rescue dog? Probably not by means of a thin body or a neglected hair coat. More commonly, the best evidence is the dog's behavior. He might be fearful and timid or, conversely, overly aggressive. He may lack social skills with other canines, or lack social skills with people.

So, you find what you think is the dog of your dreams at the local animal shelter. He's the very image of the dog you've long imagined coming home with. This makes him hard to resist. But is he the little sweetie he appears to be or is he the devil in disguise? Many inexperienced people find it hard to make a good judgment call. Sometimes they overlook problematic behavior that would be obvious to a professional trainer or behaviorist. And sometimes, even when they recognize problematic behavior they're not able to determine how serious the problem is.

Many people in this situation would benefit from the help of a professional in evaluating their potential choice. A lot of professional trainers and behaviorists are happy to perform this kind of consulting for a fee. If problems are noted, the professional can determine whether they're fixable and, if they are, can set up a rehabilitation program.

When Things Go Wrong

Let me give you a real-life example of how things can go wrong. Some clients of ours in Northwest Washington state shared their lives for years with a nice little dachshund that eventually died of old age. They wanted to get another dachshund to fill the gaping hole that the death left in their family, but they didn't want just any dachshund. They wanted it to be a rescue dog. Their choice wasn't surprising, considering how they made their living. The husband and wife did professional interventions for drug and alcohol abuse, traveling around the country to perform them. A rescue dog would seem to fit nicely with their lifestyle and values, but they wanted help in picking one out, so they came to us. My husband and co-trainer, Jason Young, had seen a dog at a local animal shelter he thought might come close to what this couple wanted, an attractive little Chihuahua/dachshund mix.

Jason evaluated the animal, determined that he was a lovely dog, and told the couple he thought it would be a great dog for them. The couple went to the shelter and met the dog, and liked him, but decided that their next dog had to be pure dachshund, like the last one. So they passed on this little guy.

Not long afterward, the couple found a rescue dachshund in California through an on-line service. They viewed his adorable photos on-line, and then fell in love with him by reading his on-line profile. They traveled together to California, adopted him and brought him home. Unfortunately, they didn't ask a professional in California to evaluate him.

After they got their new dog home, the couple realized they had adopted a nightmare. The dog acted aggressively toward people, often biting them, was nervous and anxious, destructive and incredibly vocal. Within a short time they were back at our kennel to see if we could help them. In fact, there were things we could do to help moderate the bad behavior, we told them, but we could not fix the underlying problem. That's because the underlying problem was not related to the dog's character, which is influenced by environment, but resulted from unsound temperament, which is genetic and is not correctible.

You have to admire the couple, because they're certainly not quitters. They're still living the nightmare, and apparently plan to do so for the next 14 years or however long their dog may live. They're too emotionally involved now to give up, they say.

If they had proceeded more cautiously, however, and enlisted professional help in California, they probably would have saved 14 years of grief.

Once you have determined that your potential rescue dog is of sound genetic temperament, you next need to assess his or her behavioral problems, figure out their likely origin, and develop a plan to address them. Many novice owners will benefit from professional help at this point, also. A professional can get the owner and the dog pointed in the right direction with training, and can set up a complete program that the owner can follow for the dog's rehabilitation.

Chapter 5

Preparing for Your New Companion

My dog is worried about the economy because (dog food) is up to 99 cents a can. That's almost $7.00 in dog money.

— Joe Weinstein

I had a training client in Seattle who lived in a magnificent home near the beach. She brought her new nine-week-old terrier pup home and set the pup up in a puppy playpen in the living room of her beautiful home. In the pen with the pup she put food and water – which was a mistake – and a kind of pad that you can buy in pet shops that soaks up urine. The pads are disposable, and when the puppy wets on them you throw them away.

Well, the puppy kept busy soaking up pads, and the woman kept busy throwing them away, and I assumed that this is where she intended for the puppy to relieve itself. Finally, however, in week three of our training, I asked her, "Don't you want the puppy to go potty outside?"

"Of course," the woman replied.

"Well, with the pads," I said, "you essentially have trained her to go potty in the house. When I'm housebreaking a puppy, I don't want it to go in the house. I train it to go where I actually *want* it to go."

A look of surprise came over the woman's face. She hadn't realized she could do that. I suggested how to go about it, and in less than a week, the puppy was housebroken. Goodbye absorbent pads, and goodbye annoying mess on the radiant-heat living room floor.

The lesson here is that you need to think carefully about what you want a new dog to learn, and then go right for the target as soon as the dog moves in with you. There's no point in training it first to behave one way and then to behave another.

You should be ready to begin positive training the first hour your new dog is in the house. Your dog can handle it. As a canine, he's probably sensitive to the fact that rules abound everywhere, because every pack, whether it's canine or human, maintains and enforces its own rules. If you take him to one doggy day care on Tuesdays and another on Fridays, for example, he quickly will learn the differences between the rules that the two doggy packs enforce. He's good at that. He just wants to know what the rules are.

As the leader, you should make all decisions for your new puppy or new adult dog, just as a canine leader would do. You decide, for example, when feeding time occurs, and present the food to your dog, rather than let the dog come to you and demand to be fed and have you comply. Another example: You take charge of all home security. You assess situations and declare what is and is not a threat. Those situations involve everything from mail carriers to meter readers to unannounced guests. You communicate your decisions to your dog. And you find a nice, comfortable place among the family where your dog can lie down, and you teach him that this is the place where he should do it.

It is important for a family to discuss ahead of time exactly what a new dog's rules will be. Will the dog be allowed on the couch? On the beds? Will he get scraps from the table? May he dig holes? Chase cars? Rules vary dramatically from household to household. There are no universally good rules or bad rules. What is important, and a kindness to the dog, is to communicate your rules clearly and to have every person in the house enforce them consistently.

Getting Ready for the Big Day

It's exciting to come through the door of your home for the first time with your new canine companion. But if you want the event to go smoothly, you will need to plan for the occasion. Sometime ahead of the big day, you should begin to acquire equipment, and look at your home with a critical eye to determine how you can make your dog's transition to it a smooth one.

In most cases, even adult dogs do not come with their own collar and leash or bedding or feeding utensils. These are things you'll have to prepare in advance, and we'll talk about the best way to do so.

At a minimum, you will need a collar and leash, a soft blanket that your dog can use as a bed, and a couple of appropriately sized aluminum bowls, one for food and the other for water. Obviously you will not want a food bowl that is too small for a large dog to get its muzzle into easily, nor too large for a small pup to use comfortably without climbing into it. I usually make water available for my dogs at all times, except when they are undergoing housebreaking.

Your dog should have a comfortable spot for his bed. The bed can be as simple as a blanket or a towel on which to curl up, or can be as elaborate as a commercially manufactured doggy bed of an appropriate size for the breed or breed type that you have selected.

Leashes

I recommend a six-foot leather leash for walking your dog, and also later for training. Leashes come in several sizes and materials, but training leashes most often measure six feet. Why? Because most dogs recognize what professional trainers refer to as a six-foot "domineering zone." Within it, a person can most easily influence the canine through strength of personality, and you should use that zone to your benefit by keeping your dog within it during most training. Since the goal is not necessarily to dominate an animal, it probably would be more appropriate to call this your "zone of primary influence," which more accurately reflects how you will use it to foster in your dog a feeling of responsibility to you as its leader. Nevertheless, I will continue to refer to it in this book by its common name.

As far as a dog is concerned, he's either in the zone or out of it, and if he's out of it, he feels less of a need to demonstrate responsibility to you. You can, of course, work effectively with a dog outside the zone, but that is an advanced level of obedience that reflects an advanced relationship between you and your dog.

Leashes abound in several kinds of materials besides leather, such as cotton webbing, nylon and chain. I recommend leather, because it is friendlier on your hand than other materials, a factor that becomes more and more important the bigger and stronger your dog. Leather also sends a crisper, clearer message than other materials from you to the dog. Consider your leash a telegraph line through which you will send all of your messages. You want it to be a fiber-optic line, not two soup cans joined by a string.

I like a leather leash of half-inch diameter with a light-weight clasp to attach to the dog's collar. Some leashes sport a heavy clasp, which tends to bang the dog on the head during walking or training to the point it becomes distracting. The animal will find a lighter clasp less annoying.

Cotton webbing is my second choice in a leash material.

Collars

You need something to which to attach your new leash, and that is the collar. A chain training collar of the proper size is appropriate for use during walks and while your dog is learning the rules of his new home, provided your dog is out of his young puppyhood and is at least pre-adolescent or older. Eventually you also will want a flat collar for the dog to wear when he's not undergoing training. For the youngest puppies, a choke collar is inappropriate, and a flat collar should be used.

When it comes to training collars, our goal should be to use a type of collar that imparts the lightest correction that is effective with our particular dog.

You should begin with a collar no heavier-duty than you think you will need. I recommend starting with a medium-link collar for medium to large breeds, and a fine-link collar for medium to small and toy breeds. The smallest link that will not break under the pressure exerted by your dog is best, because the finer the link, the clearer and crisper the message it sends, simplifying things for your dog.

A chain collar sometimes is called a slip collar or a "choke" collar, even though it isn't intended to choke a dog, only to gain its attention. It consists of a linked chain with a metal ring on each end. To use the collar, slide the chain through one of the rings to create a circle. As you stand facing your dog, hold the collar so that it looks like the letter "P," with the excess chain hanging out the bottom of the ring on your left, and slide the collar carefully over the dog's head. It is important that the collar be put on the dog correctly, in the "P" configuration as you face the dog, so that when you relax tension on the leash, the collar will immediately slacken. If you place it on the dog incorrectly, by holding it in the shape of the number "9," it will remain tight on the dog's neck even after you relax tension on the leash.

These instructions assume that you plan to work the dog on your left side, which is the side on which most dogs are trained to heel and to walk. If you plan to work the dog on your right side, hold the collar in the "9" position while slipping it over the dog's head.

An easy way to remember the correct technique for standard, left-side-of-the-handler work is "P" for "Perfect" and "9" for "*Nein*," the German word for "no."

When opened to its maximum diameter, the collar should be just large enough to slip over the animal's head. Most training supply stores will allow

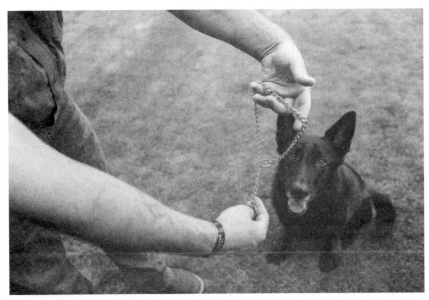

Hold training collar in a "P" configuration before slipping it over your dog's head.

you to bring your pet in to be fitted, or will allow you to make an exchange if you purchase the wrong size.

Additional Equipment

In addition to these few basic necessities, a dog crate is a wonderful enhancement to your inventory.

Is crate confinement cruel? Absolutely not. It offers a lot to a pup. It teaches bladder and bowel control, and teaches independence. It helps to show the dog that he doesn't have to be with people or with other dogs every moment of every day; that it's comfortable to spend some time alone. It helps to teach patience. Most dogs that have been properly socialized and trained to crates enjoy the safety and security of their own private den. Many like it there so much that they spend a portion of each day inside an open crate of their own accord.

If you have more than one dog, it's best that they do not occupy the same crate simultaneously, because sharing defeats some of a crate's benefits. Sharing does not encourage your dog's independence, for example, and it doesn't provide him with a private space where he can be alone when he wishes to be. You should encourage healthy independence so that each of your dogs is able to think for himself and not be overly reliant on other dogs for decision-making. Keep in mind, the goal is to develop great companion dogs, and a dog that is totally dependent on another dog in the household is a lot less a companion for you.

It's nice if you can put a blanket or a towel in the bottom of the crate to make it more comfortable for your dog. You want it to be a warm, safe place for him, and you want him to be fond of it.

Being placed in a crate never should be used as punishment as, for example, a child being placed in his room for misbehavior. Negativity or anxiety should not be associated with your crate. It is to be only a safe place.

In my house, I provide a bed for each of my dogs in his personal crate. I also provide a large bed my dogs can share in the living room and another in my bedroom. That doesn't mean, however, that you have to have that many.

If your dog rides in a car, will he do so in his crate, or do you need to consider a harness so you can seatbelt him in? In some states, the law requires that a dog be restrained in a vehicle, either with a belt or by using a crate. Even if the law doesn't demand it you should restrain your dog for his safety, because if the driver suddenly stands on the brakes, the laws of physics can launch a dog like a missile and keep him airborne until he slams into some obstruction.

At some point you are likely to need grooming supplies. Your dog's breed or breed type will govern what you need. For a short-coated dog like a Labrador, you may need just a brush. For a long-coated dog like an Irish setter, you might need a dematting rake and a dematting comb.

Is your dog of a breed that will need a haircut every six to eight weeks? If so, you may need shears. Alternatively, you may decide to take your dog to a professional groomer, and you'll have to work that into the family budget. Some people don't care whether their dog looks as though they put a bowl on his head and then cut around it. Others do care, and take their dog to a groomer every few weeks, but it's an ongoing expense.

If your dog does not visit a professional for grooming or bathing, you will have to trim his nails periodically at home, and for that you'll need a special nail trimmer designed for dogs. Its size will depend on the size of your dog. A lot of people wonder, by the way, whether they really need to bathe their dog. I recommend that they do bathe, but the frequency depends on the breed and also whether this is a farm dog or a house dog. At a minimum, I recommend that you bathe your dog once a quarter, more often if necessary. However, too much bathing dries out the natural oils that a dog needs to protect his coat.

Depending on his breed and on the climate in which you live, your dog may need a coat or a sweater to make him comfortably through the winter. Chihuahuas, greyhounds, whippets, dachshunds and Doberman pinschers, for example, don't have much hair coat or body fat. Depending on the climate, that can make life pretty chilly for them at times.

All of the equipment discussed in this chapter is available at most pet supply stores.

Getting Ready for Housebreaking

Before your dog comes home, you will want to consider where and how he will obtain exercise and also relieve himself. Do you live in an apartment or in a house with a yard? If you live in a house, is the yard fenced with chain-link or other materials that will contain a dog? Is it surrounded by invisible fencing? Does it contain a free-standing kennel? Or do you plan on leash-walking your dog to provide him with exercise and an opportunity to empty his bladder and bowels?

Dogs prefer grass or dirt where they go to the bathroom. Concrete would be the last choice, but if it's all you have you can use it. An important point: You need to keep the area clean where your pup defecates by disposing of the droppings regularly. It may surprise you, but dogs can be quite fastidious about where they relieve themselves, and if you allow an area to become littered with fecal matter, your dog may simply refuse to use it. If you ever have stopped at a service station and walked into The Restroom from Hell, you will know how your dog feels.

Years ago, I worked with training clients in Tacoma, Washington, who had an amazing house that sat on a bluff and looked out over Commencement Bay on Puget Sound. In their back yard, the portion of the home that connected with the bluff, they had an in-ground swimming pool, and the yard didn't have a lot of landscaping. Most of the yard was devoted to a concrete patio that surrounded the pool, but it did include an earthen area of about 14 feet by 14 feet that contained a few decorative shrubs.

The family had acquired a previously owned golden retriever, a lovely dog, and the shrubbery area is where they wanted her to relieve herself. The dog was happy to comply, as this 14-by-14 area was a place to which she naturally gravitated.

Six or eight weeks after they had brought their dog home, they called me to report that they had a problem with her. She had stopped using the shrubbery area, they complained, and had begun to urinate and defecate on the patio surrounding the pool. They wanted that corrected.

I asked if I could see the area in their yard that they wanted their dog to use. As I'd suspected, it turned out to be the doggy version of The Restroom from Hell. I asked the family when the last time was that anyone had cleaned up back there. The husband looked at his wife, and she looked at him, and they both shrugged. Nobody had been cleaning, and it had become so riddled with feces that you couldn't bribe, browbeat or bluff their dog into going anywhere near the place.

At my suggestion the couple cleaned the area, and the problem immediately solved itself.

Feeding

A lot of people get hung up about what to feed their new dog. That's understandable. The choices are so bewildering that you almost would have to be a nutritionist to find your way sensibly through all the alternatives that compete for attention.

A good place to begin your decision-making is with the people from whom you obtain your dog. If you acquire it from a breeder, he or she can tell you what the dog has eaten until now. If you obtain your dog from a shelter, staff members there often can provide the same information. It's usually a good idea to keep your dog on the same diet, at least until you have had time to consult with a veterinarian.

Transferring to a new home can be a source of stress for any dog, no matter what its age, so don't pick that time to change its diet. However, when you take it in for its first medical checkup, which should occur within a week or two of acquisition, this definitely is a subject to bring up with the veterinarian. The doctor not only can check your dog's health and give you advice about diet, but can recommend the type of grooming tools and other equipment best suited to your particular dog.

Keep this in mind: All dog foods are not created nutritionally equal. Your new companion deserves high-quality food, and you should be willing to pay a little more for it. At my house, we feed our dogs about half-and-half dry kibble and raw ground meat that is prepared specifically for dogs, mixing them together at meal time. We believe that the kind of food we serve is important. The kibble is top quality, providing plenty of nutrition, and the meat is not just hamburger that we pull off the shelf at the supermarket. It contains nutritional supplements and additives that are formulated especially to meet canine needs.

A veterinarian can discuss the pros and cons of various foods, and can discuss the quality of particular brands. You might ask him whether he recommends nutritional supplements with the brands that he favors.

In addition, a veterinarian might recommend puppy chow for a canine at the start of his life, a senior-type diet for a dog in his geriatric years, and perhaps a low-calorie food for a dog that's obese. These specialty foods are not gimmicks, and can be desirable for a dog at various stages of life. The veterinarian also can talk with you about appropriate amounts of food for your dog, and about frequency of feeding. At our house and in our boarding facility, adult dogs eat twice a day. However, pups may need to eat more frequently.

Remember, you are not exhibiting kindness to your dog if you over-feed him. Obesity can lead to a wide range of physical ailments, some of them serious, and can shorten a dog's lifespan. I periodically encounter clients with dramatically obese dogs who tell me, "I read the directions on the back of the bag, and I'm feeding the amount they recommended." The problem is, many packages tend to err on the side of making sure your dog gets sufficient food, rather than too little. That concern probably is compounded by the fact that dog-food companies are, after all, in the business of selling dog food.

If your veterinarian recommends a change of diet for your dog, it's a good idea to make the transition gradually. You might change your dog's kibble by starting to mix three-fourths of its current kibble with one-fourth of the new brand for a day or two. Then go to half and half for a day or two, and then three-fourths, one-fourth in the other direction. This gives your dog's digestive tract a chance to adjust.

Chapter 6

Bringing Your Puppy or New Dog Home

If you pick up a starving dog and make him prosperous, he will not bite you; that is the principal difference between a dog and a man.
– Mark Twain (1835 – 1910)

Sometimes, when we first walk through the door with our new pup or with a new older dog, we may be reluctant to make any demands on it at all, concerned perhaps that the new dog might think us too harsh. An owner often is inclined to offer a new dog a several-week honeymoon during which implementation of virtually all rules is postponed as a favor to the dog. The owner hopes this will make the dog feel welcome. Training in rules and boundaries can come later, the owner believes.

Unfortunately, what such an owner doesn't realize is that training *has* begun immediately, even if – like the training that occurred in the Seattle beach house – it isn't the training that was intended. What such training often teaches the dog is that few if any rules exist in this house. This has two effects on the dog, and both are negative.

The first effect may surprise you, and it is this: The apparent lack of behavioral guidelines in your home probably will not make your dog feel comfortable, but more likely will make it feel insecure. The fact is, dogs gravitate toward structure. They are happiest when they know the rules and the rules are enforced consistently. It doesn't matter whether they live in a human household or with a canine pack, and it doesn't matter if the rules vary from house to house or from pack to pack. Because of the way a dog's mind works, learning the rules instills confidence in the dog and provides it with a sense of security.

This is such an important factor in a dog's life that some people would view a life without training and structure as a form of neglect. Dogs that we encounter at our training facility which exhibit lots of anxiety often turn out to be dogs from living situations that lack clear structure.

The second negative effect caused by postponing rules is that when you finally begin to impose them, it may confuse the dog, because it will not understand why your expectations have changed. And, the dog may not readily accept the change, because you already have habituated it to a different behavior. Yes, you can impose new requirements through training any time you choose, but this will be harder than if you simply had imposed the rules that you wanted from the beginning. If you show your new dog from the moment he crosses the threshold all the rules and boundaries of your house, he probably will accept them as the way things are, because he's never known them to be different there.

Honeymoons don't only work in one direction, however. Dogs, too, often are inclined to give their owners a honeymoon period at the start of a relationship.

We sometimes hear from people who recently have acquired a previously owned dog who tell us that "this is the best dog in the whole world. It doesn't destroy stuff or threaten people or jump on furniture or get into the garbage."

I typically say, "How long have you had it?"

They usually say, "A couple of weeks."

What's going on here is that this is a period when the dog is most insecure. He's trying to figure out his new environment and his new pack, both human and animal. He's very much inhibited and subdued. He doesn't feel comfortable enough yet to start to take ownership of things.

It requires several weeks – six, more or less – for a dog to figure out that he lives here permanently and that this is his new pack. During that time he appears to have extra-good behavior. Often, we get to hear from these same people again at six to eight weeks, when they have gotten to know who their dog really is, and they'd like some help solving a few problems with him.

So take advantage of this canine-sponsored honeymoon opportunity by implementing rules, structure and boundaries right from the start, even for the dog that seems perfect already. As he becomes more comfortable in your home, you may observe him starting to become territorial in the yard, and with his food dish, as he comes to believe that he owns them. Perhaps now he won't allow the delivery van driver to come up the driveway anymore. Now that he's starting to feel more comfortable, perhaps he's beginning to threaten people who ring the doorbell.

As things like this evolve, you must correct them from the onset. Don't let them become habitual behaviors. If you allow your dog to threaten people at the door, for example, for weeks or months, it becomes harder to address the problem.

As your dog becomes more and more comfortable in his new home, it's important that you continue to reinforce boundaries. Your dog must know that he needs to adjust to your routine, not you to his. Perhaps you feed your dogs every night at 5 o'clock. But one day, your new dog gets hungry at 4:15 and demands his dinner. You can acknowledge that he's hungry, and give him the food. Or, you can teach him to adjust to your routine, and eat at 5 o'clock, when all the other dogs at your house eat.

Perhaps your dog wants to play with you with his squeaky toy. He brings it to you and pushes it onto you and bullies you with his presence and his toy. If you comply with his demand, you have adjusted to his presence and have encouraged his demanding behavior. You may be perfectly willing to play with him and his toy, but perhaps it should be at times when you want to play. You can tell him, "Go get your toy, buddy, go get your toy!" and that way, you initiate the play. That puts you, not him, in charge of the game.

Welcoming a New Dog

Your leadership responsibility begins the moment your puppy or new adult dog crosses the threshold of your home. Whether he's eight weeks old or eight years old, you need to establish your position right away.

Step by step, here is how I introduce a new dog to my home. I drive up to the home in my vehicle with the dog in a crate or loose in the back, depending on the dog. I exit the car first, go to his part of the vehicle and attach his leash to his collar. After he is leashed, he exits the car only at my invitation.

Next, we spend as much time together outside the vehicle as it takes for him to settle down. It might take two minutes or it might take 20. When he has achieved a settled state of mind, we cross the threshold together into the house. He still is on his leash, because that is the only way I have at this point to communicate with him effectively.

I take him from room to room on the leash and introduce him to the different parts of the house, to the people who live there and to the other pets – dogs, cats, birds. His wearing the leash is critical, because if he loses the leash I lose my ability to communicate with him easily and to train effectively.

My new dog remains on a leash 24/7, inside as well as outside the house, for at least the first week. Sometimes I let him drag the leash around the house. Other times I attach it to my belt, and have him accompany me around the house while I do chores. I need that leash to teach him the rules of the

new house. He wears the leash until he shows me he has a clear understanding of what I expect of him, whether that takes a week or two weeks or more. The time varies from dog to dog. And the learning process covers a multitude of rules and behaviors.

A similar process often is advisable, by the way, when reintroducing a dog to his home after he has been away. When a dog comes to our boarding facility for a several-weeks stay, for example, he may temporarily forget a few of the rules that he learned at home. We have our own rules and boundaries at our facility, to which the dog quickly adapts, but they are not necessarily the same as the ones he dealt with at home.

When arriving home after a visit with us, a dog typically goes overboard with excitement. Here are his old bed, his old toys, his old human pack, whom he loves. He might race around and jump up on people and appear for a while to be generally out of control. It would be a service to the dog to get him into a calm state of mind before bringing him into the house on a leash, in a controlled manner, and then gently reminding him that all the rules that had been in force before still apply.

Toy Breeds Need Tough Love, Too

Your doorbell rings, you open the door, and before you can stop your dog she charges aggressively past you onto the porch and is all over your poor visitor like a falcon on a duck.

A tragedy in the making?

Not really. Your dog's squeaky "Yip, Yip, Yip!" doesn't exactly instill fear. Your dog is a four-pound Mexican Chihuahua who just thinks she's a Rottweiler. Actually, the whole display is kind of cute.

Except, of course, in the eyes of your visitor, who probably would like to wring the little bugger's neck. Dog aggression never is cute when you're the target of it, even when it comes in a small package.

A lot of toy breeds have the reputation of being ankle-biters. Is that because they are just low-quality breeds? Or is it because of something else?

Actually, it's because of something else. Whether you have a four-pound dog or a 150-pound dog, its default setting still is a doggy brain. Large or small, dogs view the world and interpret information in exactly the same way. Sometimes, however, we fail to create enough structure for a toy breed, because we tend to overlook a lot of their bad behavior.

In overlooking poor behavior, we empower the poor behavior. The dog in such a scenario sees the other entities in its household as weak. If there aren't strong entities in the house, the dog believes it has no choice but to take that responsibility for itself. Even though it may be only a four-pounder, it becomes – in its own mind – the leader of the pack.

Dogs believe that every pack needs a leader, no matter whether the pack's members are dogs or humans or a combination of both. And a dog's default setting, regardless of its size, is to fill any apparent vacuum in leadership. This often becomes immediately apparent to us when we're dealing with a large dog. We tend to overlook it when we deal with tiny dogs. But rules, structure and boundaries are just as important for your four-pound dog so it doesn't become a nuisance to others.

Quite often we treat toy breeds like human infants. We carry them around a lot. We allow them on our furniture. We don't ask much of them, and we don't set up rules and boundaries for them. If a 150-pound Rottweiler jumps up on us, we almost always see that as bad behavior. If a four-pound Chihuahua jumps on us, we have no trouble overlooking it.

If a 150-pound Rottweiler threatens the UPS man at our front door, hopefully we tend to take notice of it. If a four-pound Chihuahua does it, we tend to see it as cute.

Small breeds are no easier or harder to train than larger dogs. The intensity of the corrections you give during training certainly will be dramatically different for a Chihuahua than for a Rottie, but you should correct for all of the same poor behaviors. You certainly shouldn't want to excuse them. All dogs need the same kind of structure in order to live satisfying lives.

In many other respects, however, living with large or small breeds is not the same. Life with each has its own nuances.

For example, a thing we have a tendency to do with toy breeds, because they're cute and cuddly, is carry them to a lot of the places they go. Although that's fun to do, and in part is why we enjoy having toy breeds – so we can cuddle them – we need to give them a healthy dose of what it's like to be treated like a real dog.

Among the dogs I personally own is a petite Mexican Chihuahua. I understand it's critical that when I take her out in the world to experience life that she experience it on her own four feet. So I intentionally take her places on her leash even though it might be more convenient just to pick her up and pack her under one arm when we're walking around.

Saturdays, for example, when I take her to the dog-obedience classes that I conduct, I might carry her during some portions of the classes. But when we arrive at the training site, she gets out of the car and walks into the class on her own feet. This teaches her to meet the world on its own terms, a skill she needs if she is to live a happy and successful life. This tiny tyke is really something to see, by the way, when she walks boldly into a class full of larger dogs, brimming with all the confidence she has attained by learning that she can mingle with the other dogs as a part of their group.

If she spent all of her time there in my arms, it very likely would send her – and maybe some of the other dogs – the wrong message.

That brings me to a question that owners of toy breeds often ask, and that is how you as the leader should react if you think your tiny dog is threatened by a larger animal.

Here is the way I handle it. In an emergency, as a very last resort, I might pick up my dog to keep her from harm. In a perfect world, however, if I saw danger approaching I would get the two of us out of harm's way simply by walking both of us out of the line of fire.

Picking up your toy breed to keep it safe sends a couple of messages you

*Even tiny dogs like this Mexican Chihuahua need
structure and discipline.*

probably aren't intending to send. One, if you whisk the toy breed off the
ground and into the air, you've just identified your dog as prey. You have in-
creased the intensity of the other dog's prey drive by doing that.

Two, if your dog wasn't already afraid of this oncoming dog, then you've
just taught her to be afraid. This may surprise you, but the message you send
when you whisk her off the ground is that you're also afraid. Where she might
have been only mildly worried before, now she's really frightened, because she
thinks you are frightened. No matter what the size of your dog, any time the

pack leader – that's you – becomes weak and afraid, your dog becomes afraid, too.

By not "rescuing" my dog all the time, I help to build her self-confidence and to build her confidence and trust in me.

Housebreaking

When you walk through the door with your dog for the first time, should you consider confining it for at least part of each day? Most definitely. Crate confinement is an excellent aid to housebreaking, and it has other beneficial uses as well. So let's talk about housebreaking, because it's usually the first thing a new owner wants to teach a young dog.

The best way to teach housebreaking is with crate confinement or constant supervision or, most often, a combination of both. If I cannot monitor a loose pup constantly, I will either put him on a leash and attach the leash to my belt, or I will put him in his crate, where he is safe from the world and the world is safe from him. If he is attached to my belt, he's unable to run down the hall and pee in the spare bedroom unbeknownst to me. If I see him start to pace and sniff the floor, I can scoop him up and get him out the door so that he has a successful experience of going to the bathroom outside.

When you take your pup outside during the training phase of housebreaking, even if it's not an emergency, it's a good idea always to carry him or to put him on his leash for the walk to the door. If you allow him to run loose, he might stop between the crate and the door to relieve himself.

If your pup relieves himself in the house, don't scold him, because it is you who has fallen short in your supervision. If you see the puppy squat, whisk him up and race him outside, repeating the phrase, "Let's go potty!" Hopefully, he'll get to finish the rest of the chore outdoors. Most commonly, the pup will turn the plumbing off when you pick him up, but you do risk the effects of a traveling leak until you get out the door.

When you get outside, take the pup directly to the same location where it always urinates and defecates, not to a new location. He'll smell the urine, and know that this is where he does the job.

Once you have reserved an appropriate place for your dog to use as a bathroom, you need to convince the dog that inside your home is not the appropriate place. Crate confinement aids in this because canines instinctively are denning animals, and they don't want to urinate or defecate where they sleep or eat. It's important, however, that you provide a crate of the proper size. If it is too small, it's uncomfortable. And if it's too big, it does not provide the feeling and the benefits of a den. The crate for any dog, including a pup, should be just large enough so the animal can walk in, stand comfortably inside, turn around and lie down. Some owners make the mistake of buying too large a crate, so the dog can grow into it. It's too large for housebreaking, however, if the pup can walk to the other side of the crate, urinate or defecate, then walk back to the original side and lie down. You need a crate that is an appropriate size for your dog at each stage of his growth. That might mean buying a series of crates, borrowing crates from friends, or getting crates from animal shelters, which sometimes offer them for rent.

A puppy can be in his crate for three to four hours at a time during the day, and also overnight, although you might want to set your alarm for an early hour the first few weeks to take the pup outside to relieve his bladder. He won't be able to hold urine as long as an older dog. Do not put water in the crate.

As part of the housebreaking regime, you should monitor what goes into the puppy and when. If you do, you'll have a good idea of what is coming out, and when. At our training and boarding facility, we feed as many as 40 dogs breakfast at 7:30 every morning, and I can tell you what's happening at 7:45. It's the same at dinner. We feed at 5 p.m., and I can tell you what's happening at 5:15. A puppy up to the age of about four to five months probably is being fed three times a day. So, plan accordingly.

If we allow our puppy to graze all day, or give it treats or snacks throughout the day, it will be harder to determine at what time it should defecate. Not that we want to withhold treats, but during housebreaking – which is just a week or two – it might be wise to curb some of that as an aid in regulating your puppy's functions during this teaching phase.

While we certainly don't want to withhold the puppy's water, I will regulate it to some degree at this time also. He will have unlimited access to water at mealtimes, and I'll also offer it each time he goes outside to potty, and this may be as many as 10 times a day. He'll have an opportunity to take a drink on the way back into the house, from a bowl outside the door. I will keep water off the floor inside the house, however, and I won't put it inside his crate. Some puppies will drink water only when they're thirsty, but some will drink just because they happen to be walking past the bowl. Others will play in it. If I'm going to go to bed at 10 p.m., I'll probably give my pup his last access to water about 8 p.m., unless it's an exceptionally hot day or he has had rigorous activity. This is not throughout his life, by the way, just during training.

Are there other methods that work for housebreaking? Yes. Actually, you can housebreak with negative training by giving your pup free run of the house and then scolding him for relieving himself indoors. But why would you do that when you can teach just as effectively and just as quickly using positive reinforcement and positive repetition?

Chapter 7

Administering Corrections

Dogs like to obey. It gives them security.

— James Herriot

When you are trying to teach a new dog the rules of your household, or trying to impart training of any other kind, the best way to do it is with a training collar and a leash. Many people underestimate the power of a collar and leash inside a house. They assume that the only time a dog needs to wear them is when it leaves the home.

In my house, any time I invite a new dog in, or establish new rules for an old dog, I put his leash and training collar on him. In this case, the leash usually will be a piece of light line, such as clothesline or even heavy cord, depending on the size and age of the dog, because he will be dragging it around inside the house. This eliminates the possibility that a puppy, or even an older dog, will chew up a fine leather leash. With a larger dog, such as a Labrador retriever, for example, you might attach a line of 18 or 20 inches, which is not long enough to trip the dog or to drag on the ground, yet provides enough of a handle to administer a correction to the dog. In the case of a puppy, the line would have to drag on the ground.

If one of the rules at your house is that the dog is not allowed on the couch, for example, the most important thing is never to invite him to get on it. However, if he should take the initiative upon himself, look at it as a training opportunity. Use the light line and collar to correct his behavior.

You should not view the dog's attempt at the couch as disrespectful to you. The dog actually needs to make the attempt so he can be corrected for it and learn from the experience.

Another behavior that you might wish to correct is accosting guests as they come through the door. Again, the light line and collar are the perfect tools for this. The same with a dog that tries to beg at the dinner table, if such behavior is against your rules.

Don't concern yourself, by the way, with issues of fairness. Is it "fair" for the rest of the family to eat at the table while the dog gets only to watch?

Such distinctions will be lost on your dog. A dog is concerned only with what a rule is, not whether it is just.

One of the rules in my house is that my four-pound Chihuahua may lie on my lap on the sofa so I can pet her. My 85-pound German shepherd dog may not. He has a comfortable dog bed on the floor next to the couch, and that is where he can relax. However, my German shepherd dog doesn't have the ability to ponder the justness of this. His canine brain doesn't work that way. He simply knows that's how it is, and he accepts it.

When Using Corrections

In order to train your dog in any aspect of life with people, you must gain the animal's cooperation. Then you must reinforce that behavior. You do this by administering corrections and rewards. When your dog makes a mistake, no matter whether he's learning to sit on command or learning not to chew people's shoes, you must administer a correction immediately. This always is done – no exceptions – with collar and leash. You know you have achieved compliance when your dog consistently performs a task or demand correctly and in a timely manner.

Some people have a major misconception about what corrections are, so let's clear it up right now. This is probably the most fundamental and important single point for you as a trainer to understand, and it is vital that you embrace it. The point is this:

Corrections are *not* punishment in the usual sense of the word. Corrections are administered simply to develop discipline in the dog, to communicate our wishes and our expectations to the dog. The dog must understand what we want before he can deliver it.

Impatience or anger must never play a part in corrections. You never should allow yourself to become frustrated or emotionally charged when your dog does not behave correctly. You should administer a correction only so the dog knows that his behavior is incorrect, and you should be very matter-of-fact about it. If you lose your temper, ultimately it will damage your relationship with the dog. Anticipating future angry outbursts from you, he may begin to mistrust you and become reluctant to work for you.

Keep this in mind: When dogs correct each other, they administer a correction and move on. They don't hold a grudge, or withhold interaction or food or playtime. Dogs don't understand that kind of behavior. If you exhibit it, the reason for it will be lost on them.

Here's something else to think about: Most of us from time to time encounter hand-shy dogs. Such dogs tell us volumes about the people with whom they live. Hand-shy dogs live with people who don't know how to correct them properly. A hand-shy dog has been spanked on the hindquarters, perhaps, or slapped on the snout or whacked with a rolled-up newspaper. That never should happen, and it doesn't need to.

Our goal is to develop discipline, never to punish, and we do it by means of corrections. Many people are not clear about the meaning of "discipline." What is it? Let me answer by describing a dog that has it. A dog with discipline knows his job and does it enthusiastically. A dog with discipline knows what behavior you expect of him, and produces it willingly. A dog with discipline knows what your role in the family is, and respects and appreciates it.

Discipline is not punishment. Don't get those words mixed up.

So, how do you administer corrections properly to instill discipline? You do it with a leash and collar. The leash is your telegraph line through which you send messages to the dog. He receives those messages through the collar. You want to provide enough correction to get your message across, no more and no less. Every dog is an individual, and will require a different intensity of correction. You administer a correction with a crisp jerk on the leash. It's not a drag, not a pull. It's a "pop." As long as the collar has been put on the dog correctly, in the "P" configuration as you face the dog, when you relax tension on the leash, the collar should slacken immediately.

How do you know how much intensity to use? Your dog will show you. Some dogs have soft characters. They don't require much of a correction. Other dogs have harder characters, and more is required to get their attention. Remember, this is not about punishment and is not about anger or frustration. This is about communication. But in order to gain the attention of a dog that's engaged in intensive misbehavior, you must meet or exceed his level of intensity.

Let me give you an example. I went to the home of a client one day to work with her small terrier. In spite of his diminutive size, this little guy was no shrinking violet. He was a gladiator in a compact package. She told me one of her major headaches with the dog was that when an animal show was broadcast on her large, flat-screen TV, her dog went berserk. He would roar challenges at the TV and, unable to attack the screen, which was mounted on a wall, would attack whatever was within reach on the floor. This might include socks and even his doggy bed, which he would take in his jaws and shake violently. Even furniture was not immune to his attacks, and his owner could not calm him or control him. His intensity was so high that food or toy distractions could not reach him.

"Okay," I said. "Let's set him up."

We put his training collar and leash on him, and took him into the TV room, where the woman surfed cable channels until she found an animal show. The little terrier went nuts, zooming on an emotional scale of 10 to about a 12. He was off the chart, jumping and pulling and snarling and trying to attack the TV.

I knew that to correct him I had to come in at his level of energy. And I knew from experience just how much energy that would be. I met him at a 12, and gave three or four snappy jerks on the leash. He immediately shut down, and turned his attention from the television screen to me as though to say, "Oh! You want me to stop attacking the TV!"

I leaned down and gave him a scratch behind the ears as though to say, "That's absolutely right, my little friend. Attacking the TV is against the rules, and it's not going to happen."

It turns out the dog was happy to comply. He had no hard feelings about the correction, because a moment later he jumped into my lap, wagging his tail. During the rest of the lesson, he showed no interest in attacking the television.

The reason his behavior had become a problem up until then was that nobody ever had communicated to him before, at a level he found meaningful, that the behavior was not acceptable.

When distractions don't work, some people are reluctant to administer a correction at a level that a hard-character dog demands. In such a case, the person surrenders his opportunity to be leader in the relationship, and the dog takes that mantle upon himself. The dog then is empowered to set his own acceptability standards. And there's nothing wrong with that, by the way, as long as you're willing to live in a home where decisions are made by a canine.

I experienced this phenomenon with a client one day when we were correcting her dog's misbehavior in her home. This was a nice dog, but quite aggressive and hard in character. It was, in fact, the pack leader in her house. We set up a scenario in which we presented the dog the opportunity to misbehave, and when it did, I administered a correction so the woman could see how to do it properly. It's part of being the leader in your home. The correction worked, and the dog lost interest in further misbehavior of the same type for the rest of that day.

The woman, however, was not pleased, and told me that she never would administer a correction of the same intensity that I had. Apparently she planned to reason with her dog.

What happened next was predictable. About a week later, she encountered my husband while dropping off dogs at one of our facilities, and complained that her dog's behavior had been backsliding. In fact, he already had resumed the specific misbehavior for which I had corrected him just a week earlier.

"The training's not working," the woman complained.

My husband knew exactly what was going on at her house.

"Have you ever noticed," he asked her, "that when you hand the leash of that dog to Dianna – in fact when you hand all of the leashes of all of your dogs to Dianna – how well-behaved and well-mannered the dogs become?

"That's no accident," he pointed out.

"And have you noticed," he continued, "how when Dianna hands the leashes back to you, mayhem takes over?

"That's no accident, either."

You may wonder, if corrections are administered only with leash and collar, how to administer them at odd moments in your home, for example when one is needed unexpectedly. In my house I do it with the training collar and the light line which a dog wears at all times it is loose in the building if it is in training and is not yet trustworthy.

Let me give you an example of how to use it. A client of mine had a young dog that lived in the house with her and, unfortunately, had not yet reached the point in its training where it was a reliable companion. One day, the woman came out of her bathroom, looked across the living room and into the kitchen, and saw her new dog standing with its front paws on the kitchen counter, trying to get food. Her immediate reaction was anger, and she hollered harshly at the dog, which jumped down and scooted away.

She told me about the incident later, and asked me why I thought the dog had done such a bad thing. She wanted to know whether she had handled the situation correctly.

I replied, "How would he know yet that his behavior was not okay? I would want him to have the opportunity to make the mistake, to be corrected for it, and to learn from it."

In my house, he would have been wearing his training collar and light line, I told her. I wouldn't holler, because then he would know a correction was coming, and I would lose a teaching opportunity. Instead, I would quietly walk up behind him while his feet still were on the counter, grab the line, and administer an immediate correction. I would teach him what the meaning of "off" is.

He has to make a mistake to learn from it, I told her, so when I see a mistake I'm not offended by it. It's not a bad thing; it's a good thing, really.

Let's take a typical leather-slipper scenario. If my young dog picks up the slipper to chew it, and I holler at him, I've only distracted him. He drops the slipper, but he hasn't learned from the experience. I know that he's going to pick it up again later. But if I walk over, pick up the line while he's still holding the slipper and give him a light pop and then redirect him to one of his toys, I've given him an opportunity to learn. I'm doing him a favor, as well as myself.

If your dog-in-training wears his training collar and line whenever he's loose in the house, we could be talking about a period of six to eight weeks. That may seem like a long time. But it's not when compared to his lifespan of about 14 years. And once his training is complete, his collar and line come off.

Chapter 8

Socialization

If your dog doesn't like someone, you probably shouldn't, either.

– Author unknown

The call came in about noon, and the caller turned out to be an official at a nearby county jail. A felon had escaped, he said, and he wanted to know if we would help round the escapee up. This happened when I lived in West Virginia, where I was attending a school that trained dog trainers. Residing at the school was one of the most talented bloodhounds in that entire section of the Appalachians, and it was this dog's help that the caller really sought.

The next thing I knew I was out in the West Virginia hills huffing and puffing up a steep ridge behind that amazing dog, which was snuffling her hound-dog heart out, hot on the trail of the former prisoner. I figured it was only a matter of minutes until she and I had this guy up a tree.

That, however, was before we reached the top of the ridge. Because when we did, that old girl stopped dead in her tracks. She melted into what we call "passive immobility," and refused to take another step. Forget about the prisoner's trail. Forget about the prisoner, in fact. She had lost him for good.

The reason? A herd of harmless cows that stood gazing dully at us from just over the brow of the hill. This phenomenal bloodhound never had seen cows before, it turned out, and her first encounter with them had just overwhelmed her.

A dog trainer would tell you that the bloodhound had not been socialized to cows, and my experience offers a good example of why it's so important to socialize your pup properly to as many things as possible while you have the chance.

Socialization is the act of introducing your pup to situations and experiences, and teaching him or her to deal with them in a calm and confident manner. It is the foundation for any dog's life, whether he's a service dog, a hunting dog or a companion animal. Socialization is the imprinting on his mind of resource material that he will use throughout his 14 or so years of existence.

Mom Is Important

Earlier, I advised against separating a puppy from its mother if the pup is younger than seven weeks. The reason for this is that canine socialization begins virtually at birth, and the party responsible for the process for the first two months of life is the pup's mother. Those first weeks are critical to your dog's proper development, and so when you bring a puppy into your home you should find one that has stayed with its mother for at least seven weeks. Eight weeks is better.

Puppies that leave their mothers prior to seven weeks of age often have multiple lifetime problems. If for some reason their biological mother is unable to nurture them for those first critical weeks, it is essential that they have a substitute canine mother, who will teach them what they need to know about being a dog.

If something interferes with this natural process – if the birth mother dies, for example, and the pup is bottle-raised by humans or is nurtured by a mother of a non-canine species – the pup will reach weaning time without having learned how to be a dog. The result is likely to be life-long communication and relationship problems with other canines.

Human beings cannot replace what a mother dog teaches. Nor can a pig or a sheep or any other non-canine.

Early Socialization Is Vital

So, let's say you come proudly home with a beautiful eight-week-old puppy that has been taught properly by its birth mother what it means to be a dog. The next eight or nine weeks of its life are equally as important. That is the time during which you must finish the job its mother began by socializing your pup to all the things that its mother didn't have an opportunity to address.

A lot of dog owners are eager to start training right away with their newly acquired companion. At Camano Island Kennels, we try to slow them down, however, and get them to focus instead on socialization, especially if their pup's age is within the critical nine-week window of seven weeks to 16 weeks.

Any socialization you undertake after that time certainly will be helpful, but it is most valuable and makes the greatest impression on the dog if it occurs between the seventh and 16th week of life. This is a special time for your puppy that you cannot get back later. Training can take place at any time, but the prime window for socialization comes and goes quickly, and you should take advantage of every moment of it. The window starts to close rapidly after 16 weeks, and although your pup still will be able to process new experiences, it will not do so as readily or as effectively as it did while the window was open. One might compare it to the early childhood period in humans during which children are able learn a language – or even multiple languages – almost by osmosis. Once that window closes – about the age of 14 years in humans – a person still can learn a new language, but never as easily and as naturally as during the open-window period.

What are the things to which you want to introduce your dog during this impressionable period? Everything you can think of. Introduce him to people, to other dogs, to farm animals and wildlife, to noise and confusion.

Dogs that aren't properly socialized to people, for example, often grow up to be biters. They may accept members of their human family but at the same time react to people outside their own pack with aggression that's based in fear. To avert this, take him where people gather. Visit parks and street fairs. See that he's exposed to different kinds of people; women and men, children of various ages, various ethnic groups. Children are a particularly important category, especially running, shouting children. If you have none of your own, borrow some. Utilize nieces and nephews, or introduce your pup to neighborhood kids or to the Little League team that plays on Saturdays in the local park.

Your pup doesn't actually have to meet all the people you expose him to. He just needs to know that they are out there; that there are lots of people besides the handful who exist inside the security of his own four walls, and that they don't pose a threat to him.

If you enjoy riding in your car with your dog, start your pup early. Some dogs get to ride in a car only once a year, to go to the veterinarian's office for booster shots. That can be quite an ordeal for all involved.

Introduce your pup to loud noises. Take him down to the station to watch the Amtrak come through. And if you're rearing a future hunting dog, you'll want to expose him to the sound of gunshots, of course.

How should you conduct your dog's exposure to new things? First, put a collar on your pup and attach it to a six-foot leather leash. This puts your pup into a controlled environment, and puts you in control of the environment. Then, think about your own behavior. This is absolutely critical, because you will tell your animal how to feel about what he's experiencing, whether it's fireworks, gunfire or a screaming ambulance. He will look to you for leadership, and will take his cue from your demeanor.

When you take him down to see the Amtrak train come by, for example, it's important that your pup see that its noise doesn't alarm you or repel you. Don't pick him up at a critical moment; your dog has to experience life on his own four feet, whether he's four pounds or 150 pounds. Your goal, however, is to redirect his mind while he's experiencing something new.

Since a dog can focus on only one task at a time, give his mind something to work on while he's undergoing the new experience. If your dog has had obedience training, this could be as simple as holding him in a "sit" position. If he's busy holding a "sit," he doesn't have the ability to focus as much on a train that may make him feel insecure. If he's not that far advanced, you can distract him by attempting to show him how to sit, or by directing his attention to a treat in your pocket or to a toy.

The hours that you invest in proper socialization when your pup is in the open-window period will pay off in many years of rewarding companionship with a stable, dependable, enjoyable canine companion. Socialization is the single most important gift you can give him. It is the platform upon which everything else in his life is built, and if the platform contains serious flaws, everything that you layer on top of it will be insecure. In a worst-case situation, you may end up with an adult dog that that will experience mild to severe limitations for the rest of its life.

For example, it may not do well with people it doesn't know. It may not do well with children and may not be trustworthy in their presence. It may turn out to be dog-aggressive. Considering that the average dog lives for about 14 years, that's a long time for you to have to coexist with such problems.

If You Miss the Window

If you do miss the socialization window, all is not lost. You still may be able to moderate the impact of a poor beginning, although it will take much more effort now on the part of both you and your dog. Let me tell you about a recent experience of mine.

As chance would have it, I got a call from two people at nearly the same time, each with a similar problem and each seeking a solution. Each was a woman in her 50s with no small children at home, and each had a new dog. In one case the dog was a 22-week-old Doberman pinscher. In the other, it was a 10-month-old border collie cross. The women, who had not met, discovered that whenever a child approached, their young dogs fired up, barking, displaying a lack of confidence and sometimes acting aggressively, although they appeared to have no problem with adults. Both women considered the behavior unacceptable.

I put their dogs together in a class of two, and I, the dogs and their owners set out to address the problem. We met one weekday at 2 in the afternoon in a shopping center parking lot across a busy street from an elementary school. I knew that the school let out at 2:10.

When that moment came, the women and their dogs and I were on the sidewalk across the street from the school, each dog wearing its training collar with a six-foot leather leash attached. The school bell rang, and kids poured out of the building like bees out of a damaged hive, shouting and laughing, waving pieces of art work, clambering aboard school buses and running to meet parents in the school parking lot. Our dogs immediately hit their alarm buttons, but we kept them on our side of the street. We walked them calmly up and down the sidewalk across from the school, and worked with them on heeling, sitting and staying.

For the next 30 minutes, kids came out of the building in waves. Little by little, our dogs returned to a more normal state of mind as they began to realize that they weren't about to be attacked. It was a great half an hour of exposure to little people, none of which we introduced to the dogs, because the dogs were not ready for that yet. They simply needed to see that there are a lot of children on the planet and that the kids pose no threat.

By the end of the half an hour we were able to cross the street and walk up and down a little on the sidewalk closer to the school. A few children still were running up and down outside the school, but by this time the dogs had had enough exposure from across the street that their comfort level had grown a bit.

I noticed that the Doberman, at 22 weeks old, was doing much better at adapting to this than was the 10-month-old border collie cross. Since the Dobie was significantly closer in age to the 7-to-16-week window of greatest opportunity, this was to be expected.

We ended our 30-minute lesson feeling we'd had a great first day, with a lot of success, although we still had a long way to go. We were optimistic now that these two canines might at least learn to tolerate kids. We knew, however, that because of their ages, these two dogs probably never will take to children the way they might have if they had been socialized to them naturally during the open-window period.

Rescue Dogs and Socialization

A lot of people assume that if a dog comes from a shelter, chances are good it has been abused either physically or psychologically. This often seems to be confirmed by the dog's behavior. However, clients often make worst-case assumptions based on canine behavior that they interpret incorrectly. For example, I have a client who adopted a rescue dog that reacted fearfully every time she swept the floor with a broom. The woman assumed that the dog had been beaten with a broom. While that's possible, it's not very likely. It's more likely that the dog simply never had seen a broom used as an extension of a person's body, and interpreted its whisking as a possibly hostile action.

While my client's assumption was faulty, it was not unusual. How often have you heard someone say, "My dog is scared to death of large men with ball caps. She must have been abused by a large man who wore a cap."

Possible? Yes, but more likely, she simply never spent much time around large men. Or, perhaps, what caused her alarm was that the bill of a cap often obscures a portion of the wearer's face. Many dogs become uncomfortable if they cannot see what a stranger's eyes are doing.

Another client acquired a 10-month-old rescue dog, and discovered that it showed fear toward many things around the home. She assumed that her dog had been abused with similar objects. I told her probably not, and I evaluated the dog and discovered that it had not been socialized during the critical time in its life when socialization is most effective. The result was that the dog was not able to process information correctly because it did not have enough life experience to do so.

The client was intrigued by my theory, but not convinced that it was correct. So, we left the rural part of our island together and headed into town with her dog in search of a more bustling environment. As we walked down a busy street, we encountered a large-diameter hose lying across the sidewalk, pumping water out of a construction site and shooting it into another area. Her dog had been doing well until it needed to cross the hose, and then it exhibited fear.

"This is the kind of reaction I've been getting at home," my client said.

"Yes," I replied. "But what are the chances that your dog has been beaten with a water hose? Probably slim to none. Chances are he just hasn't seen one in use before."

A few minutes later, we walked past a supermarket whose door was controlled by an electronic eye. We triggered the eye, the door opened, and her dog launched into another fear-based reaction.

"What are the chances he's been attacked by a door?" I asked.

Farther down the street we came to the public library. An American flag on the pole out front was whipping in the wind, snapping like a string of firecrackers. Her dog reacted as expected.

"What are the chances . . . ?"

"Ah, I'm beginning to get it," my client said.

Sometimes, people create their own canine problems when they "rescue" a dog from a shelter, bring it home and continue to rescue it far beyond the time by which a rescue should have been completed.

Here's an example of what can happen. A client of mine owns a dog that was rescued from a puppy mill, where the dog spent the first several years of her life as a professional mom and had been neglected. Because of this, the dog had limited socialization and limited life experience. But the puppy mill, as poor an environment as it was, was the only environment she had known, and when she was removed from it she was uncertain and lacked the tools and the confidence to deal with the world.

The woman who adopted her was a lovely person, full of good will and good intentions. Unfortunately, she tried to make up to the animal for all the wrong that had been done to it in its life, and so she over-sympathized with every behavioral abnormality the dog displayed. She overindulged it, coddled it and failed to create rules and boundaries for it. The result was that she inadvertently encouraged the dog's lack of confidence by daily reinforcing its own low opinion of itself.

One of the ways the dog's lack of confidence showed was that when guests came to the woman's home, the dog ran to the farthest bedroom and hid from the visitors. The woman allowed this behavior to occur and to continue, thus reinforcing not only the behavior but also the lack of confidence that prompted it. The woman didn't understand that by allowing the dog to hide, she encouraged it to hide. When we do not actively disagree with a behavior, we silently endorse it.

Unfortunately, as this continued, the dog's flight reflex became stronger, not weaker. The woman didn't realize that, when given a choice about whether to engage with strangers or with other animals, an unsure dog always will choose not to.

What should the woman have done?

She should have leashed her dog when guests arrived and required it to encounter them, even from across the room. She should neither have forced the dog on the guests nor the guests on the dog, but should have required the dog to remain in the same room with them for however long the guests were there. The point would be to show the dog that having guests in the home is normal. Eventually, the owner should have worked gradually toward expanding the experience on subsequent visits by introducing the guests to the dog or vice-versa.

Fleeing from strangers is only one of several possible problems a rescue dog might exhibit. For example, a new owner might discover that the animal is aggressive to other dogs. Improper canine socialization at an early age can lead to dysfunctional canine relationships, which can result in a dog that picks fights because it is afraid.

Another dog might display aggression for other reasons. For example, it might be one of a breed that is hard-wired for aggressive behavior. Or it might be a dominant canine that finds itself in the presence of another dominant dog. That usually creates a ruffle.

If you have an aggressive dog, you probably will need professional help to determine the reasons for the aggression. In most cases a professional can easily assist you in managing the problem. Often, that is done by exposing your canine to other dogs and properly correcting it through its leash and collar when it misbehaves.

Not all dogs necessarily like other dogs. We can't always change that. But it is critical that they learn to put up with each other. A dog that is well mannered and well controlled can tolerate the presence of other dogs, and we must insist on it, even with a rescue dog.

Chapter 9

Methods of Training

In order to really enjoy a dog, one doesn't merely try to train him to be semi-human. The point of it is to open oneself to the possibility of becoming partly a dog.

– Edward Hoagland

People can choose from among several ways to train a dog. All of them work to one degree or another, and different styles are best suited for different types of dogs, depending on breed, age, temperament, background and character. In choosing a training method, we also must consider the severity of any undesirable behavior that we might wish to correct.

Is your pupil an eight-week-old puppy with a virtually blank memory drive and no personal baggage? Or is it a dog that has come to you with years of firmly imbedded habits, including long-term behavioral problems?

Whatever the style of training you select, its goal should be to build a relationship with your dog that is constructed on trust and on mutual respect. Years ago, it was fairly common to train by forcing a dog to do what the trainer desired. People did achieve results that way, but in my opinion it didn't build the kind of relationship that most of us with our dogs.

My preferred style utilizes positive reinforcement all or at least part of the time, which is reward-based. It involves "marking" desirable behavior in such a way as to call the dog's attention to it, and then providing a reward to encourage the dog to repeat the behavior. My favorite kind of reward, when it is effective with a particular dog, is physical or verbal praise or a combination of both. Some dogs, however, do not place much value on praise, and so we must find some other reward that they do value. It might be a chew toy to mouth for a moment, or a ball to chase or even – if necessary – a food treat to gulp down. Whatever appeals to a particular dog enough to be valued highly by him becomes the dog's "currency." We reward him in that currency for a good performance in order to reinforce the desired behavior. You might say that in searching for an effective currency, the trainer is adapting his methods to the needs of his pupil.

In this chapter, I'm going to discuss a few of the popular styles of training, and talk about why and how they work.

Four Classic Psychological Approaches

First we must discuss the classic kinds of psychological approaches that teachers and trainers may use when providing instruction to any pupil, whether that pupil is a canine, a rat or a human being. The approaches are positive reinforcement, negative reinforcement, positive punishment and negative punishment. Misconceptions abound concerning what these terms mean, so let's try to sort them out.

Many novice dog owners who call our facility to discuss training are under the impression that there are two major types of training. One, they believe, is positive reinforcement, which sounds fluffy and nice, and the other, they believe, is negative reinforcement which, by its very label, sounds as though it must be bad. Keep in mind that psychologists, not dog trainers or educators, coined these terms. What some of them mean may surprise you.

Positive reinforcement is pretty much what it sounds like. It involves providing a stimulus, often a pleasurable one, to encourage a desired response or behavior. For example, a parent gives her child dessert if he eats all of his dinner. It is "positive," however, only in the mathematical sense that something – in this case dessert – is added to the mix.

Negative reinforcement is the approach most often misunderstood. It involves taking away an adverse stimulus in order to encourage a desired response or behavior. For example, a parent allows a child to skip his chores on a Saturday as a reward for good behavior during the week preceding it. It is "negative" only – again – in the mathematical sense. Something is subtracted or taken away; in this case, the need to do chores.

Positive punishment is the process of providing an adverse stimulus to discourage a certain response or behavior. For example, a parent yells at a child not to touch a hot stove. It is "positive" because something – the yell – is added to the scenario.

Negative punishment is the process of taking away something pleasurable in order to discourage a particular response or behavior. For example, a parent takes away a child's television privileges to discourage misbehavior.

In dog training, only two of these techniques commonly are used; the ones that psychologists call positive reinforcement and positive punishment.

Positive reinforcement involves using rewards to encourage a desired behavior, and implanting that behavior strongly enough that it becomes second-nature to the dog. I personally use that technique a great deal. The other technique that I most often use is what I call "correctional reinforcement," which is – in psycho-jargon – a positive punishment. That sounds harsh, but it is not harsh the way that I apply it. Keep in mind that in the example used in this chapter, positive punishment is illustrated by a parent yelling at a child not to touch a hot stove. The "punishment" aspect of this is not the possibility of being burned. The punishment is the warning issued to the child not to touch the stove. It certainly is not "punishment" in a sense that any normal lay person would understand it.

I use correctional reinforcement to "mark" undesirable behavior in order to call attention to it, and then communicate to the dog that the behavior is unacceptable. Often, depending on the situation, the most effective training involves a combination of both techniques, positive reinforcement and correctional reinforcement, and it usually is heavier on positive reinforcement, or rewards, than it is on corrections.

Optimally, if we are working with a young pup that has no emotional or behavioral baggage, a positive-reinforcement approach always will be our first choice. Unfortunately, however, we sometimes encounter badly behaving dogs that need training, sometimes as a last-ditch effort to prevent abandonment or even euthanasia. In such cases, corrections can be used successfully to obtain control over powerfully motivated behaviors that may be so ingrained that positive reinforcement will not override them. In some cases such as this, correctional reinforcement actually can help to save a dog's life.

It is essential to understand that neither technique involves actual punishment in the usual sense of the word. Common understanding of the word "punishment" implies that someone has done something "bad," and must be reprimanded for it. In my world, I don't look at things that dogs do as "bad." Dogs do what dogs do. I look at those things as teaching opportunities. When I work with a dog, it is important to me that I never come from a frame of mind in which I punish. I come from a frame of mind in which I teach.

Let me tell you about a client whose experience illustrates the way in which we commonly combine positive reinforcement with correctional reinforcement in real-life situations. She came to our training center several years ago with a dog that had very nice temperament and character but was quite out of the client's control. The dog behaved badly around the house and did not respond well to directives. She also was a member of an often assertive breed, and she acted aggressively toward other dogs.

We determined that one of the reasons she behaved badly was that her training was inadequate. The inadequacy appeared to stem from the fact that she placed no real value on anything as a currency. Contributing to this was that her owners – wanting to be good owners – freely gave her abundant amounts of unconditional love, praise, toys and food treats. None of these things was bad, per se, but she got so much of everything – without earning it – that she didn't appreciate it.

After studying this dog, we determined that she actually got quite a bit of enjoyment from playing with a ball. What we needed was for the owners to increase the value of this in the dog's eyes by ceasing to make it available so freely. We needed them to sensitize the dog to the ball as a desired reward, and then to bring it out at appropriate times when the dog had earned a reward. With our coaching, the owners did this successfully, and we were able to use the ball as a currency – a positive reinforcement – to enhance the teaching of this dog in obedience exercises.

Unfortunately, the ball did not work in correcting the dog's aggressiveness toward other canines. Her compulsion was so strong that the reward incentive did not override her desire to fight. She had practiced her aggressive behavior for so long that it had become a reflex action that did not involve any conscious thought. So in regard to this problem, we used correctional reinforcement. We marked the negative behavior with leash and collar, and used verbal communication – teaching her the meaning of "no" – to make her understand that the behavior was unacceptable.

The eventual result was a success story. The dog finished its lessons with us as a super-good family pet, its old behavior finally discarded and new and more acceptable behavior adopted to take its place.

Clicker Training

"Clicker training" is a type of positive-reinforcement training with an extra step. In it, the handler operates a metal device to produce a "click" at the same time a desired behavior is performed. He also provides the animal with a reward. The theory behind clicker training is that as a dog learns to associate a click with a reward, eventually it will perform the desired behavior just for a click when the reward is withdrawn. The click becomes the reward.

Many professional trainers use this type of teaching when preparing to compete professionally with their own dogs. It takes considerable practice in order to perfect timing with clicker and reward. Many pet owners express interest in this style also, but many others seek a simpler style that they can use without the need to develop the critical timing required when using a clicker.

If clicker training is something that interests you, I recommend that you and your dog attend at least a basic course in the subject with a professional trainer to get started with a proper foundation in it.

Desensitization

Desensitization is another offshoot of positive reinforcement that can be appropriate in some circumstances. It is the process of associating positive experiences with a person, place, thing or activity that formerly created anxiety because the animal never was socialized properly to it. Continuing exposure to the anxiety-inducing object or experience, properly combined with appropriate reward, can allow an animal to form a new response to that particular stimulus.

In desensitization, one tries to create a good experience for the dog. This usually is done by increasing the dog's exposure to the situation or the environment in small increments so as not to alarm the animal unduly, and by combining the exposure with the reward.

Desensitization is not to be confused with a technique known as "flooding." In flooding, one places a dog in a situation or an environment that intentionally causes the dog intense anxiety, and keeps him there in an effort to override his stress.

Although flooding can work in some situations, it usually is employed only in extreme cases. Desensitization is a kinder, more humane way of achieving the same goal, and should be your first choice when appropriate. However, there are relatively rare cases in which flooding might make sense, but only with the approval and advice of a professional. I'm aware of one case, for example, in which a Rottweiler was scheduled for euthanasia because its phobic reaction to people resulted in fear biting. The dog presented a serious hazard because a fear-biting Rottweiler is, after all, not the same as a fear-biting cocker spaniel. Lesser remedies had not worked with this dog, so flooding was attempted as a last resort before euthanasia to rid the dog of its phobia, and it was successful.

Social Learning

Another sub-category of training is social learning, which can be an effective tool. It involves a dog mimicking or modeling the behavior of another dog. Social learning can work well with the help of a good canine teacher. Alternatively, it can produce poor results in the presence of a poor teacher. We often see the results of this type of training when a pet owner acquires a new puppy to join a resident adult dog in the home. The results will be positive if the resident dog is a well-trained, stable member of the family pack. However, the results can be quite negative if the adult dog has many bad habits or is emotionally unstable.

A good example of this occurred to one of our clients whose dog belonged to one of the herding breeds. This happened to be an unsound dog, and when the owner wanted to add a new puppy to the mix, I cautioned him against it, because this adult resident dog was going to be the teacher for the new pup in the family. Not only did our client get one puppy, however, but a year later he got another. Now these two pups, while not actually unsound themselves, also exhibit unsound behaviors. All three dogs are nervous, over-aggressive, anxious dogs.

Reinforcement

My preference is to provide a positive training experience for both handler and dog. The idea is to structure a relationship of trust and mutual respect between handler and dog, teach the handler how to assume the leadership position in that relationship, and then demonstrate to the dog what the handler – its leader – desires from it. Most canines are hard-wired to respond to a leader – whether canine or human – in a positive way, and therefore the proper foundational relationship between handler and dog is essential to successful training.

Obviously, one cannot lecture a canine about one's expectations. A handler must demonstrate his expectations in ways that make sense to the dog. Sometimes, the most common-sense way to deal with undesirable behavior is with correctional reinforcement, so that the dog understands that its leader is directing it to cease and desist from the behavior that has prompted the correction. With a normal, stable dog, it usually takes few corrections to get the point across, and the dog usually is willing to comply once it understands

what the leader wants. Leash-and-collar corrections are reminiscent of how dogs naturally correct each other and function among themselves.

Other times it is possible to use positive reinforcement to encourage desirable behaviors, and this is my first choice whenever appropriate. My favorite positive reinforcement is an expression of approval through physical or vocal communication. The farther one strays in training from approval and corrections, the farther one gets from the way dogs naturally behave with each other. While a food reward may be effective in some circumstances during training, it should not be continued at the same frequency after training is completed. We may use food to teach, if necessary, but we do not want to have to use it for the next 14 years to get our dog to sit.

Dogs usually learn best when they learn in a manner for which they already are behaviorally hard-wired. And I prefer to communicate with my dogs not with cheese treats or mechanical clickers, but rather in a more natural way, with vocal inflections and body language. While I consider my approval one of the most desirable and effective currencies to use most of the time, however, it may not work in every case. No single currency does. In that event, a trainer must be flexible and resourceful.

Chapter 10

Finding Your Dog's Currency

Man is an animal that makes bargains; no other animal does this – one dog does not change a bone with another.

– Adam Smith

How do you motivate a dog to learn? You "pay" him with something he wants. That thing that he wants is his "currency."

A tidbit of food is a type of currency that many dogs recognize and accept, and a lot of trainers use a bit of cheese or a piece of dried liver to motivate their pupils. But many other kinds of currencies are available as well. For some dogs, an effective currency might be an opportunity to play with a tennis ball or a tug toy. For others, an effective currency might be petting and praise. Sometimes, a dog's reward can be the simple pleasure he gets out of a job well done. Consider, for example, a member of a retrieving breed who just loves to bring back a thrown object or a downed bird, or the assertive member of a breed noted for police work who gets to bite the padded arm of a person during protection training.

No matter what currency you find works best with your dog, I recommend sticking with that currency and not switching among several with the same dog. You can use praise alone as a currency, and praise can be combined with almost any other currency, such as toys or treats. But I would not mix use of toys and treats together with the same dog, for example. I would use one or the other, because that provides consistency for the dog, and adds value to the currency as well.

While many dogs recognize and accept food as a currency, in many cases a trainer can find a better motivator than food, depending on the dog. Yes, you can teach a dog to sit by using cheese. The method does work. But keep this in mind: The quality of the effort you get from a dog often depends on the type of motivator that drives him to perform the work. You often get better performance from an animal that desires to please – and to receive approval from – its leader. These desires spring directly from a canine's instinctive need to belong to a pack.

How can you best determine the optimum method to use with your dog? You can begin by considering the natural tendencies of the particular type of dog with which you are dealing. Is your dog a type of hound? Is it an assertive type of canine that might be used for personal protection? Is it a herding dog? A retriever? If it's a mixed breed, what do you think might be the combination of heritages from which it springs?

Dogs are highly individual creatures, just like people, so it is foolish to paint with too broad a brush. We often find exceptions to the general rule. Still, an assessment of your dog's breed (or its primary breeds in the case of a mixed-breed animal) is a good place to start in trying to determine effective currency, and you need to be willing to be flexible in your approach. While I'm not a devoted fan of using only food incentives, for example, some types of dogs – such as hounds – sometimes do comparatively well with them, so food might be a good place to start in trying to find a currency that will work for your beagle.

A hound, by the way, is a dog – usually with long, floppy ears – that often makes its living tracking other animals by means of a scent trail that animal has laid down on the ground (as opposed to scent that is pulled from the air). These types of hounds have many hundreds of thousands more scent receptors in their heads than do most other types of canines, and the most important thing in a hound's world tends to be its olfactory system. Scent-trailing hounds tend to be less concerned than other dogs about obedience tasks and more concerned about what they smell or taste. This does not make them "bad" dogs. They simply are bred to operate with different priorities than, let us say, herding dogs.

Canines with a tendency toward high prey drive (the desire to chase things that move), such as a Doberman pinscher or a Rottweiler, for example, often will work hard for an opportunity to chase a tennis ball.

Working and herding dogs, such as Australian herding dogs or German shepherd dogs, tend to have a tremendous willingness to please their owner or handler. A show of approval from that person often is a very adequate and effective currency.

Your Labrador retriever might work for the same kind of reward, or he might work even better for an opportunity to chase a ball or a stick.

Having considered all of these factors, then, how does a trainer determine the best currency to use with a particular dog? He does it by observation, followed by trial and error. Does your dog trip over his own feet to get to you to

(1) get to that cheese that you have in your pocket or to (2) get to that tennis ball you have in your hand or to (3) just get to be with you and bask in your presence? You determine this by observation and interaction. And you create simple tests involving all of the possible currencies, and then observe your dog's reactions.

How to Use Currency

Having determined what currency to use, determining how best to use it also is a process of trial and error. At the beginning of training, we want to make an association for the dog between the behavior we desire and the reward we intend to bestow. So, during this phase we will make our reward more readily available so he can see the connection between it and the behavior we desire.

Once the initial connection has been established, however, a trainer must determine how much of the currency is appropriate, how much is too much, and how much is not enough. Obviously, we must use enough of the currency to give our dog the satisfaction he is trying to earn with his performance. However, the more one receives of something the less one tends to value it, and if a trainer is too liberal with a dog's currency, the currency becomes less effective. After the connection is firmly established, you probably will not want to use the currency more often than once after every third to fifth successful repetition.

How you disperse your currency must be individualized for the particular dog. I could pull 10 dogs out of our boarding facility from among those who are here for training, and would find a different amount of currency optimum in each case. Let's say, for example, that each of the 10 is motivated by praise. I probably would give each of them different amounts of praise, a different duration of praise and a different type of praise, all depending on a particular dog's personality. With one, I might want to scratch him behind the ear or pat his side while I tell him what a wonderful job he has done. With another dog, I might just have to say, "Ah, good job!" with no physical praise attached.

Dogs are as individual as people. Some are very touchy-feely, others less so. Let's say I'm working with a happy-go-lucky golden retriever which is very affectionate. Maybe he is a dog that appreciates a lot of physical praising and touching. Another dog might prefer just a simple tickle behind his ear, or only a verbal "Attaboy."

The amount of currency you pay, whether it's verbal or physical, must be individualized to the particular dog. You determine whether you're doing it correctly by the results you are getting. As a trainer, you have to be flexible. It's like driving a car. As you drive down the road, sometimes you need to apply a little more gas, and then a little less. When you start down a hill, you might take your foot off the accelerator and coast for a while. If you start to pick up too much speed you might even touch the brake. Working with a dog is much the same. At times you may want to provide a little more reward, at other times a little less. You have to pay attention, read your dog, and read the results to determine what is correct.

When your dog is performing your demands on cue, without any lag, and is showing a desire to perform for the reward, you know you are headed in the right direction.

Remember, dogs are not instinctively verbal animals. So if you administer verbal praise, it has to be more than a lackluster "Good boy," delivered in a monotone. If you do that, you might as well text-message him. Instead, say the words as though you mean them. Put some emotion into it. Make sure your pride in him shows in your voice. It's your tone and your body language that matter, not so much the words.

If you want to get down on one or both knees to praise your dog, by the way, that's all right. You gain no advantage by staying on your feet. A dog will not interpret your getting lower to the ground in any negative way.

The way to use a toy correctly is to keep the dog on his leash and give him about 30 seconds of playtime with the toy by rolling it to him or tossing it lightly in the air and letting him catch it. Then the toy goes back in your pocket.

Timing

Whatever type of reward you administer, its timing is of utmost importance. Regardless of the type of currency, you have approximately three critical seconds within which to mark the canine behavior you want to reward (or to discourage). About three seconds, maximum, is all the opportunity you have to bring the dog's attention to the behavior. Taking less time is even better. Anything in excess of three seconds, and the window of opportunity is closing.

Does this mean that you interrupt training in order to reward the dog for a job well done? You interrupt training, yes, but you do not interrupt a particular task. Let us say, for example, that your dog is learning to sit on command, and that your dog's currency is an opportunity to retrieve a thrown tennis ball. You should toss the ball for him upon his completion of several successful repetitions of carrying out the command, and within the critical three seconds of having completed the final repetition.

Early in his training on a new task, you will reward him after every successful repetition. As he begins to excel at the task, you will request more repetitions from him before offering the reward. This goes back to a currency's value. If you offer too much of it, the currency loses value. When your dog has completed his training, you might offer a reward only at the end of an exercise rather than at the performance of every successful repetition or series of repetitions.

Every professional trainer has his or her preferred currency, which he will use as his first choice if it happens to be effective with a particular dog. Different trainers favor different methods, and most of the methods work to one degree or another. My preferred currency is praise, if it works with the particular dog with which I'm dealing. The use of food or a toy can be an effective way to teach if a particular dog is not impressed by praise.

However, it's important to understand that once training is completed, a handler who has been offering food should reduce its use to a minimal level. Whereas in training it might have been given for every successful repetition, it is not appropriate to give a dog a snack every time it sits on command for the rest of its life. To do so changes the character of the gift from a teaching aid to a bribe, and bribery is not a technique that dogs use to motivate each other. If you condition your dog to expect a treat every time he responds to a command, you may discover that when you run out of treats you run out of discipline, too. On the other hand, developing a dog's willingness to please results in a strong and reliable working attitude because it taps into the dog's instinctive need to belong to a pack, either canine or human. Most canines are inclined by instinct to perform tasks that their leader, canine or human, sets out for them.

Chapter 11

Preparing for Training

Dogs are not our whole life, but they make our lives whole.

– Roger Caras

Now you are ready to begin training, and the most important thing you bring to training is the proper attitude. It is absolutely critical.

You must come in the door with a friendly but no-nonsense demeanor which broadcasts that this is work time. You do not need to be loud or overbearing. Dogs are masters at reading the subtle signals we send with our body language. If you simply exude a quiet confidence and assertiveness, they will pick up on it.

You don't have to be big and brawny, by the way, to make this kind of an impression on your dog. It doesn't matter whether you are male or female, young or old, large or small. You could be physically disabled, in a wheelchair, let's say, with limited mobility and perhaps limited strength. But if you can project the confidence and the mental strength that is necessary, you can train your dog successfully.

Remember: only two possibilities exist, and you and your dog will fall into one of them. The first possibility is that you are in charge, and your dog will learn what you want so it can enjoy your approval. The other possibility is that – in his mind, at least – he is in charge, and your approval doesn't matter. How you relate to your dog will make all the difference.

But what if you're a person to whom projecting confidence and authority does not come naturally? How do you project it then? I'll try to explain by describing someone who does it right.

Imagine that she and her dog go somewhere together. The handler enters a room or an event or a situation – it doesn't have to be enclosed by four walls – and she walks in not tentatively, but with the kind of presence that says she owns the situation or the event. Let's say she has arrived at a busy street fair or a farmers market. She walks in as though it's her fair or market, and proceeds to take control of any interactions that present themselves. It doesn't matter whether the interactions are with other people or with animals. If a person approaches her, for example, the dog handler will control her own location, her dog's location and how she, the handler, interacts with the person who approached. The handler will not allow events or situations just to happen to her. If a situation presents itself, she will take control of it.

Let me give you a real-life example, although a rather radical one. Two of us instructors were teaching a group class one morning at a local park. It was to be the first lesson for a new class, and we had about 10 people and their dogs lined up side-by-side across a grassy field.

Suddenly, from the top of a hill across the street, a territorial Siberian husky spotted us from his front yard, and decided to extend his territory to our side of the street. He raced down the hill and across the street, running full-out for our group. I glanced at our students, and could tell from their body language that everyone was worried. Their dogs were worried, too, because their owners obviously were. Each person hoped that the Siberian hadn't focused on him, because it clearly was coming to fight. Each person hoped the intruder would choose some other victim.

The other instructor, who happened to be my husband, saw this start to unfold, and as the Siberian approached at high speed, my husband suddenly spun toward the dog, let out a roar, and charged at the dog like a bull bursting out of a rodeo chute. It was so unexpected that it hammered the Siberian's panic button. The dog nearly turned himself inside-out switching ends. He raced back across the street, up the hill and into the safety of his yard, his ears pinned back and his tail between his legs.

The effect on the people in our class was instantaneous. Their bodies relaxed as they realized that a dog fight had been avoided. Their dogs saw it, too, and the message it sent to them was powerful. The dogs realized instantly and without a doubt that my husband was the leader – their leader – at the park that day.

This was a good teaching opportunity, and Jason and I explained to the class what had happened. Each owner had had a chance that day to be a hero in the eyes of his dog, and nobody had taken advantage of it. In a nutshell, that missed opportunity illustrated the reason why these people were there in the first place.

Granted, this was an unusually dramatic event. But these sorts of opportunities come up every day, all day long, on a less-dramatic level, and some owners overlook all of them.

Leadership Must Be 24/7

Let me give you a more typical example. Recently I drove to the home of a client couple for my first weekly training session with them and their three small terriers. An off-leash dog park lay along my route, not far from their home. After I got to their home, I talked with the couple about the goals they wanted to achieve with their dogs. One of their complaints was that when they took their dogs to the park, it required nearly an hour to get there.

I said, "What? The park is just a block and a half away. Why does it take you an hour?"

"Because the dogs stop to smell and pee on everything," the woman said.

"Who's in charge of this walk?" I asked. It was clear it wasn't she or her husband.

"Let's go to the park," I said.

So we saddled up, and out the door we went, each of the dogs wearing its training collar and leash. This time, I took charge of the dogs, and in about five minutes we were at the park.

"This is the difference between a situation happening to you," I told them, "and you taking charge of the situation.

As the leader, you are in charge of your dog. You exercise authority over everything he does. Your dog expects this, and finds comfort and security in it. You need to adopt this attitude in every facet of your relationship with your dog. You can't be a leader on Monday and Tuesday and not on other days. You can't be a leader at home and in the car and not on the street. You're either a leader – all of the time – or you're a follower. You have to be the leader in the classroom, in the car, at home, everywhere you go with your dog.

Demeanor

Let's talk briefly about the demeanor required of a good trainer. You want a teaching style that projects calm. You want to take advantage of a dog's strengths and help it to compensate for any weaknesses. In any type of training, you must rein in your own ego and hold it in check. Dog training, by its nature, can be frustrating at times. But you can allow no frustration or anger to intrude on your training sessions. If you feel either emotion coming on, you must put down your leash and revisit training at a later time. All good trainers do this.

Communication

People tend to lean heavily on verbal communication with each other and also with animals. But words are not a type of communication that dogs use or rely on. Dogs pay attention instead to body language, tone of voice and energy level. If my body language or energy level is not assertive, I transmit that information to the dog.

An example of this occurred recently with a beginning student in one of my group classes. We were teaching her young dog a sit-stay, and this was as new to the owner as it was to the dog. She was unsure of her teaching ability, and when she attempted to give a command, she did it as though it were followed by a question mark. So it wasn't really a command at all. It was only a suggestion, and that is the way her dog correctly interpreted it.

Dogs read very subtle signs that we often broadcast without realizing it. The fact that the woman raised the pitch of her voice at the end of each command was evidence that she herself believed it was only a suggestion, and the dog detected that.

Our tone of voice or the way we stand or move speaks volumes to our canine friends. If we stand with shoulders slumped, head down, unwilling to make eye contact, we project the opposite of assertiveness. Some people are naturally – probably genetically – shy or submissive. Such a person may not necessarily lack confidence. He or she may be a very competent professor or mathematician or mechanic. But if he or she doesn't project assertiveness, a dog interprets this as weakness or vulnerability. And, being hard-wired for hierarchal relationships, when a dog detects vulnerability he has no choice but to try to take advantage of it. Where a dog sees vulnerability he sees opportunity.

At my house, for example, my house dogs always have been well behaved, because we run a pretty tight ship. But when I became pregnant with twins, the situation started to change in the last trimester of my pregnancy. I was essentially on bed rest. My husband, Jason, would go to work in the morning and leave our two dogs at home with me, and in those final days they began to run amok. The reason for it was no mystery to me. As far as leadership was concerned, I always had been a very capable person, but I wasn't when I was nearing the end of my pregnancy. In terms of leadership, I essentially had checked out, and the dogs were starting to take advantage of me.

The funny thing was, when Jason came home in the evenings our two dogs transformed into their usual sweet selves, and they remained so until he left for work again the next morning.

It wasn't until our twins were about 12 weeks old that I started to catch my breath, and the old me began to come back. Right about then, the leader in me started to check back in, and as soon as the leader reappeared, so did my two well-behaved dogs.

I talked with a woman one day who had a German shepherd puppy that needed training, and as we chatted on the phone she mentioned that the dog would listen to her husband and her son, but not to her. She believed this had something to do with their deeper male voices.

I knew from experience that this was not the issue. Her husband and son could have their vocal chords removed and they still would have more control over the dog than she. Then, in the course of our conversation, the woman mentioned that she was afraid of dogs – all dogs – including her own puppy. She undoubtedly projected that through her lack of willingness to engage.

We had to fix her, not her vocal chords. We had to fix how she felt about her dog. We had to convince her that she had the ability to be in charge. If we couldn't convince her, we couldn't help her.

How do we teach people to project assertiveness? At Camano Island Kennels, we do it through one-on-one coaching and practice, practice, practice. There isn't any one exercise that's specific to assertiveness, because myriad things are involved.

When a student pays attention to this aspect of what we teach, it's remarkable the kind of results that are possible. We had a gentleman in one class to whom we spent six weeks teaching assertive behavior so he could assume leadership with his two dogs. They were large dogs. He was a meek, easy-going kind of a guy, and he probably tried to avoid conflict. Not that he necessarily was afraid of it, but I think he just preferred to avoid it. How many of us like conflict, after all?

Some time after he had completed our course he returned to our training center to thank us. He said the class had dramatically improved not only his relationship with his dogs, but also with people he supervised at work. One of the men he supervised had practiced behavior that indicated he might be a bully, and our client had given the bully far too much leeway. As soon as he set up clear boundaries for this employee, he said, it transformed their relationship for the better.

Where Should You Train?

As you prepare to train your dog, it's important to think about what kinds of places to pick for training sites. To do that, you should ask yourself what your goals are for the dog, and in what kinds of locations your dog will have to perform the skills you are teaching.

A lot of people want their dog to be well behaved no matter where they take him, whether it's to the park, to a family reunion, on a camping trip, traveling or even to spend a day at the office. If your agenda sounds something like that, then you have just answered the question about where to look for training sites. The answer is, "everywhere."

If you train in only one location, which could be your back yard, for example, or at the training hall down the road, then expect it to be the only location where your dog will perform. Instead, start with a variety of sites right from the beginning. Maybe you'll train the first day in your back yard, then the next day in the park down the street, then maybe the next day in a remote corner of the parking lot at your grocery store. You should take the dog to sites everywhere you go in the normal course of your life. That should include into businesses that allow dogs to enter. In the town near our main training facility, several businesses allow dogs to come in, and we take advantage of the opportunity to train there, and not just in one, but in all of those that allow dogs access. If you plan to take your dog to work with you at your office, that's definitely a place where you need to train as well. A lot of construction workers take their dogs to work with them, so they need to train occasionally at construction sites.

If you want a nice companion dog with a lot of flexibility, a dog that can go to the railroad station with you to pick up friends, who can stay in hotels with you when you are on the road, who can attend meetings between you and your clients, then those all are locations where they must train. This principle is called cross-contextualization.

Distractions

You also must incorporate distractions into your training, because later you will expect your dog to perform when potential distractions occur. I routinely hear newer students report that their dogs seem to be making good progress with training, but the moment a distraction is introduced all the success falls apart. That produces a lot of frustration for the students; sometimes, even anger.

Let me tell you about one of my training clients. She and her very intelligent, five-month-old Doberman pinscher pup had started taking once-a-week lessons from me, and then practicing the dog's skills the other six days of the week. They both had been in training for about two weeks. My client called me and reported that her puppy seemed to be learning, but as soon as the woman introduced any significant distraction, all of the compliance she had attained went out the window. The woman was beginning to become upset, because in her view the pup was disobedient. I asked her to describe one of these experiences.

She had been working the pup on heeling, sits and sit-stays, she said, and decided to bring her three-year-old Doberman into the picture. The puppy was, of course, excited to see her dog friend. The woman also introduced a ball into the equation. As the adult Dobie bounced around the yard chasing the ball, the puppy went wild on the end of her leash, jumping and trying to join in the play with the ball. At that point, my client had a hard time just controlling the dog, let alone training her. When she called me she was frustrated, angry at her pup, and ready to give up.

So, what had the owner done wrong? Nothing. The pup's behavior was right on target, given its level of training. The only mistake the owner made was to become so frustrated that she was ready to throw in the towel. I advised her to continue to work the puppy under distractions at the next training session, and to keep doing so until she got the desired result. She simply had been ready to give up too soon.

I also suggested that she might reduce the intensity of the distractions until her puppy began to work well in their presence. The first distraction had been the adult dog. She added to its intensity by also bringing out a ball.

"We need to approach this in baby steps," I told her. "Bring out the three-year-old, and master working under that distraction first. Then maybe you can increase the distraction by bringing out the ball for the three-year-old to play with. You were just getting a little ahead of yourself."

The woman viewed her pup as disobedient. But the pup was not. Her owner just hadn't trained her yet to ignore serious distractions. I reminded the woman that every time we see undesirable behavior, it's an opportunity to teach a new way of doing things. We have to be presented with a situation to teach the puppy what it should do in that situation.

Should you train your dog alone, or with other dogs and trainers? Both can be beneficial. You don't have to train with others for good results, but it's certainly not harmful. One of the advantages of it is that it helps to create potential distractions for your dog and gives you the opportunity to work through them. The only possible disadvantage is that if your dog is having a serious problem with distractions, it might be better to begin your training distraction-free. Some people and their dogs will attend group classes right from the start, and that's not a bad way to go. On the other hand, if you and a friend decide to train your dogs together, there's no harm in waiting until your dog has gained some basic skills before you introduce your friend and his dog into the mix.

Participating in an obedience class, like these dogs, provides built-in beneficial distractions.

How Long Should You Train?

Training sessions should run about 20 minutes, give or take, depending on the attention span of your particular dog. You want to end each session on a high note. You do not want to work your dog so long that he is psychologically worn out. It may surprise you, but training to perform simple tasks such as sitting and lying down is a major mental workout for your dog. Think about it this way: After working all day in the woods, a logger usually goes home at night exhausted. Meanwhile, a computer programmer who sits at his desk all day in a climate-controlled office may go home as fatigued as the logger. In his case it's mental fatigue, but it's just as real as the other kind.

A dog usually operates primarily by impulse, not putting much thought into the things he does. In training, however, he must focus, concentrate and implement a thought process that governs his behavior. By the end of a long training session – especially a session that runs a little too long – your dog may feel the way the computer programmer does.

If you like, you can train once a day. When your schedule permits, you can train two or more times every day. Each session still can be about 20 minutes long, but you must be sure your dog has several hours between sessions to recover his mental freshness.

It's best not to train while your dog has an overly full stomach. A dog's senses are keener and he's more inclined to want to work when he hasn't just stuffed himself with a large meal. If you normally feed your dog twice a day, don't skip his breakfast because it's a training day. But do not feed him and then train immediately afterward. Wait an hour or two.

Professional trainers find that canines learn best with repetitions of four. Three repetitions are not enough, and five are too many. Trainers call the four-reps system "maxi-quad." It helps dogs to learn fast and to retain information for long periods. If you are working on sits, for example, you would work him in a repetition of four and then perhaps take a break of a minute or two. Use the break to play briefly with the dog or allow him to drink or just give him a rest. Then go back to work for another four repetitions.

You also can use the method by doing four repetitions of sit, for example, then four repetitions of down or some other command, then back to four repetitions of sit. The switch from one skill to another serves in place of a rest. Down the road, of course, you don't have to do everything in repetitions of four. You use the maxi-quad system only while teaching.

If you mix up the repetitions, your dog will have the ability to work for the full 20 minutes without a break. But remember: Always end each session while the dog is doing well. If your dog's performance becomes sloppier, it's an indication you have pushed the session too long. Shorten up in the future. You want the lessons to be fun for your dog.

After a training session, it can be useful to give your dog what I refer to as "dark time," in his crate perhaps, where he can absorb what he has just experienced. The term "dark time" does not imply that the dog's environment is without light. It simply refers to a rest period during which the dog does not receive excessive mental stimulation. This enhances the learning process, and is better than turning him loose to play right away. Twenty or 30 minutes of dark time is about right.

Rewards

By the way, I want to reiterate that when training, it's important to impart both corrections and rewards within three seconds of the behavior you're trying to highlight. Anything past that, and the opportunity has eluded you. This is such an important principle that it deserves strong emphasis. That's why it would be ideal to reach your dog while his paws still are on the counter, as in the example in Chapter 7. Even allowing a full three seconds to pass before administering a correction or a reward is pushing the envelope. It takes some practice to get your timing perfected, but soon it will become automatic.

Something to keep in mind, especially with praise: Sometimes people offer praise for much too long a time after the behavior that prompted it. As a result, it is less effective. You really have to mark the behavior with your praise. If you go on too long the dog certainly will enjoy it, but he won't understand why he is getting it.

Chapter 12

Basic Obedience Training

It takes a strong-minded human to appreciate a strong-minded dog.
— Mary Webber

The information you are about to receive in this and the immediately following chapters will provide you with far more benefit than you may expect. On one level it will enable you to teach your dog specific skills that you will find useful for the next 14 years or so. But more importantly, when properly applied it will provide you with a solid foundation for the entire relationship you are about to build with your dog. It will establish you as the leader in your relationship, will accustom your dog to looking to you comfortably for direction, and thus will affect how you and your dog interact in almost every aspect of your lives together. The significance of this on your daily lives will be profound.

Loose-leash Walking

The first skill you will teach your dog is to walk on-leash in a civilized manner without pulling your arm from its socket. You will use leash corrections for this, but you may wish to incorporate food or toy rewards in the training as well.

Start the lesson by standing with the leash in your right hand in front of your body, about waist high. You will control the dog through the leash with your right hand, administering corrections with that hand as needed. It doesn't matter whether you are naturally right-handed. Corrections will be a crisp jerk of the leash, followed immediately by a few inches of slack.

The collar should be right up under the dog's chin and high behind the ears, where corrections will do the most good with the least effort. If the collar slides down over the large muscles of the lower neck, the dog will be harder to control. When that occurs, slide the collar back up to its proper position while you pet and praise him.

The goal is to administer corrections with just enough energy to gain the

With leash in right hand, waist high, prepare to step out for loose–leash walking.

dog's attention, no more than that and no less. The amount of energy required depends on the size and the personality of your dog. Obviously, you would tend to use more energy with a Labrador retriever and less with a toy breed, more energy with a dog of hard character and less with one of soft character. Experience will teach you quickly the proper threshold with your dog.

Keep your dog focused through use of the leash and collar with your right hand. If his attention wanders, use the leash and collar to refocus him on you. Use your free left hand for additional focusing. Tap his muzzle lightly with the fingers of your left hand, for example, when you step out. This will keep his attention on what you are doing.

I prefer to administer this training without food or toy rewards. However, if you wish to incorporate a food or toy reward into the training, hold the reward in your right hand close to the middle of your chest so your dog, who has interest in what you are holding, is looking up at it. Switch the leash to your left hand, and hold it in front of your body, about waist high, approximately in front of your belt buckle. You now will administer corrections with your left hand.

Practice walking – not heeling, just walking – with three to four inches of slack in your leash. If the dog leaps ahead or stops to sniff correct him with a snappy jerk of the leash. Don't just pull. Then return immediately to a loose line.

If using a toy or food for focus, walk six or eight steps and then give your dog a tidbit or reward him by allowing him to play with the toy for about 30 seconds. Place the toy or a treat in your right hand again, and repeat the same procedure. You should practice this for four repetitions. After the fourth repetition, you and the dog should take a two- or three-minute break and then resume with additional repetitions, four at a time. During your break, interact with your dog, but do not offer him a reward. You want him to retain his interest in it as a pay-off for good performance.

Walk at a brisk pace, so the dog has less opportunity to become distracted. No matter where you train, it's a good idea to walk in circles if possible, at least in the beginning, and the circles should be counter-clockwise so the dog has to concentrate on you to keep out of your way. It doesn't matter how large the place where you train, if you walk in straight lines, eventually you will have to do an about-face. It is more efficient and less distracting to the dog to walk continuously in a circle.

Take your dog to train at first in places where he will experience no

Walk at a brisk pace with a few inches of slack in the leash.

If correction is needed, administer a brisk "pop" with the right hand.

distractions. But plan to use a variety of such places. If you train only in your back yard, for example, that likely is the only place your dog will perform. If your dog is typical, he should begin to understand the concept of loose-leash walking the first day.

Heel

After your dog has mastered walking on a loose leash, it is time to teach him to heel. This command means that the dog not only walks without pulling, but that he stays directly at your left side. Give the verbal command, and immediately step off on your left foot. If he becomes distracted, use the leash and collar to keep his attention on you, and to correct him if he leaves his proper position on your left. Use crisp jerks, not long pulls, and give him immediate slack after each correction.

Again, you can use the toy or food here, if you wish, to encourage his co-operation, as you did in loose-leash walking. Your dog gets the toy or the treat only when he has performed correctly. It takes some practice to juggle the dog, the leash and the food or toy, so be patient with yourself.

Walk in counter-clockwise circles with the dog on your left. Control your dog with the leash, and transmit corrections with it while using the left hand to signal the dog or to tap its muzzle gently for encouragement. If you are doing one 20-minute lesson per day, an average dog should be able to get the concept of heeling fairly well understood by the third day. If you do more than one lesson each day, the number of days required probably will be fewer. Dogs are individuals that vary greatly in their ability to learn, however, and if your dog takes a couple of days longer to learn this or any other skill, it's not cause for concern. This is just the most general of guidelines, to give you some idea of what reasonably to expect. On the other hand, if you are wrapping up a week of training on this skill and your dog shows no progress, you need to re-evaluate your teaching methods.

Sit

After the dog has learned to walk on a loose leash and at heel, it is time to introduce the "sit" command. Go into the sit by giving the verbal command and pulling straight up on the leash. This often triggers what is known as a

To teach "heel," give verbal command and step off on left foot.

"thigmotactic reflex," which causes many animals – including humans – to push against a push and to pull against a pull. In this case, it inclines the dog to lower his haunches and pull downward, in a direction opposite the pull of the leash, easing him into a sit. When he sits, immediately release all tension on the leash and praise the dog, or reward him with food or a toy.

If you prefer not to use a leash in teaching this skill, the proper technique is to hold the dog's collar with one hand and with the other hand gently push the dog's rump into a sit while using the "sit" command. In this style of teaching, the dog is likely to resist the pressure on his rump – that thigmotactic reflex again – and a trainer should not be surprised if this occurs. You simply must overcome the resistance. When the animal is seated, you bestow the reward.

You can combine "sit" training with the walking exercise now by directing the dog to sit every time you come to a stop. Give the verbal command, and if he complies, reward him with praise, food or toy. If the dog does not comply, provide him with an immediate correction by pulling up on the leash and then praising him for a sitting response.

If the dog sits and then breaks the sit in the early phase of training, give an additional command and an immediate correction. Once the dog has grasped the principal of this exercise, however, do not repeat the command if he breaks the sit. Instead, provide only a correction. Once he clearly understands the command's meaning, he also must understand that the command is a directive, not a request. Repeating a command in an effort to gain compliance turns it in the dog's mind from a command into a plea.

When you combine sit training with walking, your dog may protest your pull on the leash by stepping backward at the stop before sitting. If this happens, your instinct may be to take a step back in order to maintain position beside the dog. Do not do that, however. If you move to where the dog is, it will be of huge significance to the dog. He will have signaled you what to do, and you will have complied. You must signal *him*. Using leash and collar, require him to step forward and take his proper position beside you. You are the leader, and he must come to you. He will understand the implications of this.

Work on these commands for as many sessions as necessary, until the dog is comfortable with these routines and performs them almost flawlessly. Each new skill that you teach, starting with heeling, must be built on the firm foundation of the skills that went before. If you try to progress before that foundation is laid properly, the entire training effort eventually will collapse.

To induce dog to sit, pull up on leash, which encourages dog to lower its haunches.

Your dog should have the "sit" concept formed in the first couple of days, if you provide one lesson per day. By the end of day three, he should have a pretty firm foundation in the skill. If not, re-evaluate what you are doing. Again, this is just a general guideline to give you a reference point in assessing the pace of your progress.

By the way, when your dog is in training, seven days per week of lessons are optimal, but not critical. If you choose to train only five or six days a week, that will work. Two days off in a row will not set your progress back significantly.

Sit-Stay

Now that the dog walks well at heel, and consistently sits on command, you introduce the "stay" command, going into it from the sit. Say the command, and accompany it with a simultaneous hand signal, which consists of the left hand placed briefly in front of the dog's face, palm toward the dog. After giving the command, take one step away from the dog on your right foot, continuing to maintain control through the collar and leash.

Stay means no movement, so you should correct for movement of any type. Your concern is not only for movement that involves traveling, but for movement that doesn't, such as scratching or moving from a sit to a lie or a stand.

Upon giving the "stay" command and stepping away from the dog, it is important to step off on your right foot. When you teach the "heel" command, you lead off with the left foot, the one closer to the dog. After giving the "stay" command, you step away on the foot farther from the dog. Keep this in mind: We humans can use our voices for commands, or we can use body language, or both. Body language can encompass the entire body, used in almost an infinite number of ways. Remember, you have four extremities, not just two, and dogs are aware of that even if we may not always be. So use all of your tools. When you and your dog have become a polished team, he will know by which foot you step off on whether you expect him to move with you or to remain in position. If you are consistent – and that means 100 percent of the time – your dog eventually should be able to heel or to stay, as appropriate, without any verbal or hand signal from you. The signal will come from your feet.

To teach "stay," give the verbal and hand command and immediately take one step forward with the right foot, pivot to the left 180 degrees directly in

Give verbal "stay" command and "stay" signal with left hand, and step off on right foot.

Pivot to face dog, and maintain light contact with dog through leash held over dog's head.

front of the dog and stand facing him, leash still in your right hand. Hold the leash over his head, about the height of your shoulder, and keep just a bit of tension on the leash to encourage him to remain in position. You do not want to choke the dog even slightly. You want him only to be aware that he is in physical contact with you. While you're in front of him, use your peripheral vision to see what the dog is doing. Don't make extended direct eye contact, because that can pull him right out of the stay. If he starts to move, administer a correction immediately, in the usual way. After a few seconds, return to his side, and walk him out of the stay, leading off, of course, on your left foot, and immediately give your reward. Do this in repetitions of four, and then move into some other exercise for four repetitions before returning to sit-stay.

If your dog makes mistakes at first, do not become impatient. Look at the dog's mistakes as training opportunities. He has to make a mistake and receive a correction for it to learn.

At this point, do not try to incorporate down-stays or stand-stays into the training. You need to polish the sit-stay first, and develop a foundation that is 100 percent firm before you throw any variations at the dog. Begin to put the dog in sit-stay and move away several steps, leading off on the right foot. Wait briefly, then return to the dog's side and walk it out of the stay, stepping out on the left foot. Practice this until the dog can hold a stay for three to five minutes. Remember, you give a reward only for a correct performance.

If you praise him while he's in stay, do not incorporate his name in it. As with eye contact, if you use his name at this time, he is likely to think you want something from him, and may walk out of the position in order to come to you.

After your dog has demonstrated dependable consistency with the sit-stay while you stand in his general proximity, it is time to leave him in a stay while you gradually move farther away. You begin sit-stay training by taking only one step away from the dog before turning to face him. After he has mastered that, you move to the farthest extent of the six-foot leash. At this point, the dog still is within our six-foot circle of dominance, so the training should not be too difficult. If he needs correction, step immediately to him, administer the standard correction with collar and leash, and place him back in a sit.

The average dog should have a pretty firm understanding of the sit-stay concept by day three of its work on that skill. Expect it to be really dependable, at short range, in a week or less.

Down

The next concept is the down. It is the most submissive posture you can demand from a dog, and you may at first encounter some reluctance on his part to comply. The down may be easiest to accomplish using food or a toy. You stand facing your dog with your reward in one hand, then lower that hand to the ground and give the down command. Your dog likely will follow that hand to the ground with his nose. As he does, you place your other hand on the dog's back and guide the dog gently toward the ground, simultaneously withdrawing the hand with the reward slowly along the ground away from the dog. This often encourages the dog to creep after your retreating hand,

Ease dog into "down" from a walk by giving verbal command, gripping leash close to collar and pulling dog gently toward the ground.

and as soon as his body hits the ground, you provide him with the reward. You should practice this in repetitions of four.

Another technique is to walk your dog in the "heel" position, and place him into a down while in motion. Grasp the leash beneath the dog's chin, close to the collar, using your down command and pulling him into the down position with the leash as you come to a stop, taking advantage of his forward momentum. Once he is down, immediately present a reward.

After the dog becomes comfortable with this, teach him to go into the down position from various other positions – moving, sitting and standing – and mix them up. If you teach always from a sit, for example, the dog will learn it that way and think he has to go into a sit before the down.

Down-Stay

Next step is the down-stay. As with a sit-stay, a down-stay means no movement, including non-travel movement. Put your dog into a "down," give the verbal "stay" command and hand signal, and step off on your right foot, pivoting left 180 degrees. Keep only slight tension on the leash, just enough so that your dog will know it still is in contact with you. Too much tension may pull the dog right out of its down.

Try to move back to your dog's side before it breaks the stay, then walk it out of the down-stay and praise it for its work.

The "down" should take about three days for your dog to master, and the down-stay another three days. Training should be easier now, because your dog already has learned the concept of "stay." Also, a down-stay is a much easier position than a sit-stay for your dog to hold, because it is belly-to-the-ground. A dog is more likely to break a sit-stay on impulse, to chase a squirrel, for example, because he's already halfway standing. In a down-stay, he still may opt to chase the squirrel, but he has to think about it first. Because of this, a down-stay is by far the most reliable position if you need to park your dog for a while in a safe location.

In these and other aspects of basic obedience you slowly should introduce different levels of distraction during training, increasing the distractions as the dog's performance gets better and better. You can do this in a couple of ways. One is to enlist the help of an assistant to walk by where training is under way. That serves as a potential distraction to the dog, which may be taught with leash-and-collar corrections that during work sessions he must ignore

Give verbal "stay" command and "stay" signal with left hand, and then step off on right foot.

distractions and stay focused on you. On some occasions the assistant could provide other kinds of distractions by, for example, asking questions of you, hammering a nail, bouncing a ball or any of an infinite number of things.

Another way to train for distractions is to move some sessions from your distraction-free fenced back yard, for example, into the front yard where the dog will be exposed to passing vehicle traffic, foot traffic, children on bicycles and so forth. You can control the degree of distraction by beginning such training in a part of the front yard farthest from the street, and eventually end up doing more advanced lessons right next to the street. Public parks and shopping center parking lots also offer opportunities. In a parking lot you can start out in a remote corner of the lot, and several lessons later end up close to a supermarket entrance, where a lot of traffic moves in and out.

If the dog's attention starts to wander, correct it immediately with leash and collar to refocus it on you. When you regain the dog's focus, provide it with the reward you have chosen.

When your dog is performing all of these skills consistently well on a six-foot leash, repetition after repetition, you and your dog have successfully completed basic obedience training.

Now it is time to move on to intermediate obedience training.

Chapter 13

Intermediate Obedience Training

Yesterday I was a dog. Today I'm a dog. Tomorrow I'll probably still be a dog. Sigh! There's so little hope for advancement.
– Charles M. Schulz (1922 – 2000) (Snoopy)

In the preceding chapter, you learned how to take an untrained dog and successfully introduce it to behavioral concepts aimed at making it a valued member of the family pack. Teaching the "heel," for example, benefits you not only because your dog no longer is dragging you down the street, but also because it teaches the dog that he must look to you for information about what to do next. This sense of responsibility begins to carry over to many other aspects of your dog's life, thereby producing a valued, dependable companion.

Now you will reinforce and polish the dog's behavior so you and he or she become a smoothly running team, not only when the dog is on-leash, but – more importantly – when it is off-leash as well.

The most important thing you have tried to accomplish in basic obedience training was to lay a firm foundation for what comes afterward. In order to accomplish this, it was vitally important that at each stage of training, starting with basic, you moved in baby steps. You learned that you must allow your dog to master each small increment completely and confidently before moving on to the next. Speed is your enemy. Tiny incremental changes are your goal. Remember, you are dealing with a doggy brain, which works differently than yours. Because your dog can consistently perform a skill at a distance x number of feet from you, does not mean you can expect him to do so at a distance of x plus 10.

Long Line

When your dog is working well with you six feet distant, it is time to leave the six-foot domineering zone and graduate to a longer line. This, in effect, comprises moving from basic obedience training to intermediate. You don't need anything expensive for this. A length of clothesline will do, perhaps something you already have hanging in your basement or garage. Still using the training collar, replace the leash with the longer line, and begin to move in tiny increments beyond the six-foot range.

Uncoil the line behind you as you go and, if you wish, lay it on the ground. The line is not there for use in administering corrections, because you are now too far from the dog to do that effectively, and the line no longer is vertical or nearly vertical over his head. The line is there only to allow you to control him if he decides to move off in another direction. You would do so simply by taking hold of the line or stepping on it. If the dog decides to leave, he can't move terribly fast or far while dragging 25 feet of clothesline. At this stage, if he begins to break his sit-stay, you need to get hold of the line, step back to him as quickly as possible and administer a correction in the standard way, with a distinct jerk on his collar from a position over his head. You have no more than about three seconds to get to the dog and administer a correction if it is to be effective. Less time is even better.

Gradually increase the distance between you and your dog, no more than five or six feet at a time, after your dog has shown repeated and consistent compliance with your directions at the last distance. As in basic obedience training, your goal is to build a strong foundation for this skill, so training must be spread over many days as you master each new distance individually before moving on to the next. Remember, practice in repetitions of four, and then give your dog a short break or a change of pace. Do not extend a training session beyond your dog's limited attention span. Quit the lesson while your dog is doing well so you can praise him and end things on a high note.

The sit-stay is one of the most important skills you will teach your dog. Often, people see their dog beginning to understand the concept in the early stages, and they impatiently jump ahead and move off some distance from the dog. This is a serious mistake. To a dog's mind, this is like a different exercise entirely. You must be sure your dog has completely mastered the skill at the six-foot distance and will hold it 100 percent reliably 100 percent of the time before you move beyond that range. Then you increase the distance only gradually, in modest increments of five or six feet, attaining 100 percent perfection at each distance before moving farther.

You should have many, many successful repetitions at each level before you move the next few feet farther away. If at some point the dog's dependability appears to slacken, slow down your rate of advancement, or actually go back to a lower level and bring him up again, more patiently. Your dog will clearly show you where his level of competence is by his failures and his successes.

Out of Sight

Eventually, after you have extended your dependably consistent "stay" skill level to the farthest extent of your line and even beyond it, the next step is to move entirely out of the dog's sight. You can accomplish this by going around the corner of a building, for example, and expect him to hold the stay where you have left him. It is the most advanced level of sit-stay possible. At this level of training, it's often useful to incorporate a friend or family member into the effort. He can alert you to trouble if you have moved out of sight, or can administer a correction to the dog himself if necessary. Either tactic works.

If an assistant is not available, a good way to approach such lessons is to reduce the actual distance at first between you and the dog. Say, for example, you have taught your dog to remain in a dependable stay at a distance of 25 or 30 feet, or even more. Place your dog five or six feet from the corner of a building, put him in a stay, and step around the corner just out of his sight. You can trail the long line after you on the ground as a way to monitor your unseen dog's behavior. Start with very brief stays before you reappear around the corner of the building. Walk your dog out of the stay, and bestow your reward.

Because of the short distance that actually is between you, your dog will be able to hear you and to smell you even though it can't see you, and so will be quite aware of your presence. This should help to steady it and to encourage it to maintain its position. Gradually increase the length of time in the stay until your dog can consistently maintain it for at least three minutes virtually 100 percent of the time. Then in subsequent sessions, you can begin very gradually to increase the actual distance between you and also the amount of time you leave the dog in the stay.

Your going out of sight is a whole new ball game, however, and firming up your dog's skill on that level can take several weeks. Remember, this is not a race, so take your time.

You know your dog has mastered a particular level of sit-stay when he consistently holds it for three minutes or longer for many consecutive repetitions. Of course, you must keep your dog's attention span in mind, and never layer on too many repetitions at a time in training.

Only after your dog has achieved 100 percent reliability with his sit-stays, should you begin to call him out of a stay, rather than returning to him to walk him out. But you should attempt that only with a dog that is 100 percent reliable 100 percent of the time. During the training phase, always return to your dog, walk him out of the stay and offer your reward.

Sit-stay and down-stay are two of the most valuable skills you can teach your dog, and ones that you very likely will use in real-life situations more than almost any other. Here's a common scenario: Let's say, for example, that you return to your sport utility vehicle with a large cartful of groceries. You open the back of the vehicle, and you need to transfer all of the bags of groceries from the cart to your car. Your dog had been riding in the back of the vehicle, and you need to keep him out of harm's way in the busy parking lot. You would put him in a down-stay while you work, either outside of the vehicle or inside the back of it.

Length of Stay

How long can we reasonably expect a dog to hold a down-stay after its training is complete? A professional trainer may reply, "Indefinitely."

Let me tell you a true story about a down-stay I observed in Europe. Several years ago, when I was beginning my studies as a dog trainer in Germany, I happened to be at a specialized dog-training center one evening where a veteran trainer was working his dog. They were training under the lights, such as one finds at some U.S. baseball stadiums. The man put his canine, a beautiful German shepherd dog, into a down-stay on the field, and then strolled across the field to a nearby gasthaus to share a few tankards of beer with friends. While he drank beer in the gasthaus, the weather outside turned to rain. Every so often, the trainer stood up and looked out the gasthaus window to check on his dog. He could see that the animal obviously didn't like the rain. It repeatedly shook its head to keep water from running into its eyes. The weather clearly was a large distraction to the dog. Nevertheless, it continued to hold its down-stay on the field.

I happened to have followed the man, whom I knew, into the gasthaus, and I saw the whole situation unfold. Inside, the man continued to consume beer with his friends while they talked about dogs and taxes and a few of life's other important things. Outside, the rain gradually turned into a downpour.

And still, the dog held his down-stay.

Several more beers into the evening, the trainer finally called it a night. He bid his friends farewell, walked out of the gasthaus, climbed into his car and drove to the next village, where he lived. His wife saw him come through the door of his home, and said, "Where's our dog?"

You might call it a classic senior moment. The man did an about-face, got back in his car, drove back in the pouring rain to the field in the neighboring village, and there was his dog, still patiently holding his down-stay in the soggy field.

This man probably shouldn't have been driving a motor vehicle that evening. And he certainly shouldn't have forgotten his dog in weather such as that, or in any weather. But he most definitely should have been training dogs – which he'd been doing for nearly all of his life – and he had given this dog a really solid foundation in the concept of "stay."

Distractions

Just as you did during basic obedience training, you should continue to expose your dog during this intermediate phase to potential distractions. After all, when you and your dog are using your obedience skills together later, in real life, potential distractions often will occur all around you. If your dog is to perform well under those circumstances, he must train for them.

As training progresses and your dog becomes better at his skills, the kinds of training distractions you provide can be intensified. For example, you might decide to take your dog to a street fair one day, and work him there. Start training half a block away from the fair, within sight and sound of it, and see how well your dog does at that location. If he does well, close part of the gap. If he does not do well, you might not even go to the fair that day. It depends on the dog. Don't be in a hurry. A dog's obedience training is not complete until he can perform every skill successfully in the face of serious potential distractions.

Pace of Progress

The dog will show you how fast he's capable of progressing, and you cannot rush the process. Patience is more than a virtue; it's a requirement of the dog-trainer's job. Let me give you an example of how it works.

By end of training, your dog should be able to sit or carry out other directives even in the potentially distracting presence of other dogs and people.

A few years ago, I met a beautiful black Labrador retriever that was afraid of gunfire. This is not a sterling quality in a hunting dog, so her owner asked me to cure her of her gun-shyness. I thought, what better place to become accustomed to gunfire than at a shooting range? So I put her in my car and drove her to a large, county-operated shooting range about an hour away. We got to the range, and I pulled into the parking lot and shut off the motor. Gunshots rang out from the firing line about 50 yards away.

I had planned to get the dog out of the car and put her through obedience drills in the parking lot while gunfire rattled in the background. But I could see that she was experiencing considerable anxiety because of the noise. I could have said to myself, "We've driven more than an hour to get here. We've got to get out of the car and do some work!" Instead, she and I just sat in the vehicle with the windows cracked, and listened to the sound of the shooting. She could clearly see that the shooting did not upset me. After 30 or 40 minutes, we drove home.

The obedience drills in the parking lot didn't get done that day. Was our session a failure? Hardly. I considered it a successful training day. I could see when we arrived at the range that she wasn't ready for more than what we did, and you can't rush progress. If I had pushed it farther faster I might have made her problem worse. As the days passed, we returned to the range several times, and each time we did more together there than the time before. Bottom line, her therapy was slow but ultimately successful. She was able to return to the hunting field with her owner. But patience was of the utmost importance. With a dog, you cannot cut corners.

Commands

A word here about verbal commands: The important thing is that you always give exactly the same command for a particular behavior, and that every member of your household does it exactly the way you do. I usually suggest that people sit down as a family and decide what the commands ought to be, and then post them on the refrigerator so everybody is using the same command for the same purpose.

For example, if our dog jumps up on us, do we say, "Down"? Or do we say, "Off"? You might say "Down," somebody else in the household might say "Get down," and your dog might take that to mean "lie down." There are no right or wrong command words. But you want to have a thoughtful process for choosing them, and all members of the household need to be consistent, not only with each other, but also with themselves.

Let me illustrate what I mean with the story of Max. He was a pleasant, mixed-breed dog with great intelligence whose training had been excellent. Unfortunately, sometimes the demands his owner placed on him were beyond even his exceptional abilities. Despite being highly intelligent herself, his owner made mistakes because she didn't consider the differences in the workings of human brains and canine brains. Without being aware of it, she expected her dog to understand English. Max is a smart dog, but that's a lot to ask.

For instance, the first time the woman issued her command, she did so properly. "Sit," she said. When she didn't get the response she wanted, she modified the command. "I said, 'Sit!'" The third time, she used a string of other words. "Dammit, Max! I said, 'Sit!'"

Pity poor Max, because English is not his native tongue. Yes, dogs can learn to recognize words and respond to them. But when you string them together in sentences, that's too much.

You should use exactly the same command for a particular behavior every time. You don't want to use "Sit" one day, "Sit down" the next and "Sit down right now!" the day after that. This can be a particular problem within a family. Part of the family may use "Sit," others may use "Sit down," and still others may say, "Max, sit down." Such lack of consistency in a household sets a dog up for failure. As far as Max is concerned, everybody is saying something different.

It's best, by the way, to use the command alone – without the dog's name – for most commands. "Sit," for example, to elicit that response. "Down," for example, or any other word you wish to use consistently, to command the dog to lie down. The words themselves have no meaning for the dog except the meaning that you teach him.

It's best to attach the dog's name only to a few commands, such as "Come." People often attach the dog's name to demands for various behaviors and, unfortunately, also to reprimands. "Max, bad dog! Max, get off the sofa! Max, knock it off!"

Instead, try associating Max's name only with good things: "Max, want to go outside? Max, want to go for a ride? Max, what a good boy!" You want to program Max so when he hears his name, he feels like a million dollars.

You want him to hear that name and not be able to get to the source of it fast enough.

If you've made all the right associations in Max's brain, the command, "Max, Come!" should fill him with desire to go to you.

Ongoing Training

One further point about obedience training: In any household with a dog, training never stops. It is ongoing for the rest of the dog's life to keep him at peak performance. Generally, dogs need periodic reminders about their responsibilities, so consider it normal with your dog. Also, you need to be very conscious of your own behavior as leader in order to broadcast the messages to your dog that you intend to broadcast. You already are aware that whatever your dog learns from you he learns through repetition. What you may not be aware of, however, is that he may learn a lot of things from you that you had not intended to teach.

Let's look at Max again to see how this commonly plays out. Max is a pleasant dog with a winning personality. He's lived with his owner for several years, and she knows he has a clear understanding of the command, "Sit."

His owner decides that this is an appropriate moment for Max to hunker his hind-end down on the ground, so she looks him in the eye, makes sure she has his full attention, and utters the command: "Sit." Max stares back, his long, pink tongue hanging endearingly out of the side of his mouth, the appearance of a good-natured doggie grin on his countenance. And he ignores the command.

"I said, 'Sit!'" his owner says. Max just continues to grin.

Her frustration is growing now, because she believes that Max is disobedient. She raises her voice.

"Dammit, Max! I said, 'Sit!'" She takes him firmly by the collar, but before she can force him into the "sit" position, he sits all by himself. They've been through this scenario before, and it invariably makes her angry. She doesn't want a disobedient dog.

But Max isn't necessarily a disobedient dog. He's an intelligent one, because he's just shown her that he can count.

What Max's owner doesn't realize is that she has taught him – through repetition – that she will not enforce her command until after the third or fourth time she says it. That is the only time, Max has learned, that she will follow through and compel him to carry her wishes out. So, why should he sit any sooner? Apparently, she's not serious the first several times she demands it.

What Max's owner should have done was correct him immediately after the first command by pulling up on his collar, pushing down on his hindquarters, and putting his fanny in an actual "sit." She should have done the enforcement directly after she gave a command if she didn't get an immediate response. And she needed to do it every time. She needed to teach Max – through repetition – that if he didn't comply on the first command, a correction always would follow. Always.

Chapter 14

Advanced Obedience Training

When a dog runs at you, whistle for him.
            – Henry David Thoreau (1817 – 1862)

Finally you've come to the highest level of canine obedience training; the advanced level. What is it? It's a combination of two things. Advanced obedience training is, first, the process of completely mastering and totally refining the skills acquired in basic and intermediate training; of taking those skills to higher and higher levels of dependability.

Second, it's the acquisition of two additional skills that are too complex to deal with during the basic and intermediate stages of training. The identities of these latter two skills might surprise you. They are coming when called, or "recall," and walking at heel off-leash.

Many people think that coming when called, in particular, is a very basic command, and ought to be one of the first ones a dog learns. In fact, however, it can be one of the most challenging to teach, and that's why it's one of the last ones you should undertake. The reason for its difficulty is that failure or success at it will relate directly to the kind of relationship you have with your dog. By delaying training in this skill until you have firmly established your leadership role, you help set the dog up for success.

At my training center, I often get calls from people inquiring about training who say, "I've got this dog, and he's a pretty good dog, but I have just one complaint. I need him to come when I call him."

That may seem like a simple thing to the caller. But I have to find out how broken his relationship is with his dog to determine how much success we will have with this goal and how quickly it will come. Sometimes, when people request this, the obstacles to it can be almost insurmountable. First, we have to repair everything in their relationship that's broken, and sometimes that can be a lot. Usually, if a person contacts me because his dog won't recall, I know a lot about their relationship even before I ask my first question.

The good news is that most dogs gravitate naturally toward leaders, and so all of the other obedience skills that we have been teaching have set us up for success in this endeavor. A dog will come, or recall, only for an individual it respects and whom it clearly views as a leader. If you have gotten this far successfully in your training regimen, you obviously are headed in the right direction in your relationship with your dog. A dog appreciates strong leadership, and our dog probably is heading now down the path of viewing us differently than he did before our training began. Our dog is learning that being with us is being in a strong, safe place.

Here's a good rule of thumb to keep in mind: At this stage of your training regimen – the advanced stage – if the training is going to work for you and your dog it should work easily. If lessons are not going well at this point, it is evidence of a significant relationship problem.

You can deal with this in either of two ways. One is to go back to basics, and bring your dog up again, working along the way on identifying and repairing any problems you detect in the relationship. The other way is to refer yourself and your dog to a professional trainer or handler for an evaluation. A lot of owners assume when they do this, by the way, that they're having their dog evaluated. But the professional, if he or she *is* a professional, will evaluate both of you.

There's no shame in this. If a person truly is interested in mastering advanced training of any sort, I suggest they seek out a professional for critiquing or coaching. All professional trainers I know, including myself, go to other professionals. I often trade that service with professional colleagues when we are in the final stages of preparing a dog for serious competition, for example. I will go to them with my dog for their professional input on our performance and they, in turn, will come to me with theirs.

The most complicated relationship a professional trainer may have with a dog may be with his own, because even a professional can find it difficult to look at his relationship with his own personal dog objectively. That's why I think every person seeking to teach his dog new skills at the advanced level should seek coaching.

Come on Command

That being said, let's talk about teaching the concept of "come." You'll start with your six-foot training leash. You will introduce the command, and then reel the dog in like a fish, to your front, so that you're face-to-face. When you get him in front of you, you'll put him in a seated position and reward him with his currency for the successful performance.

Don't be in a hurry to remove the leash. You want to build a strong foundation, here, as with everything else, and you'll do many repetitions on your six-foot leash. At some point, when your dog appears to have a solid grasp of this, you'll replace the leash with that 25-foot line. Again, at this point you will move outside of your six-foot domineering zone, and when you step outside of the zone, things become more challenging.

You should keep your commands business-like but pleasant. Remember, you are not begging him to come, you are instructing him to. But you want him to desire to do it. Can you demand that a dog come? Yes, I've seen people do that, but if a dog is off-leash and you're barking commands, there's only about a 50-50 chance he will obey. When he does, it may be reluctantly, belly to the ground, ears back and tail held low. It's much more effective, and more dependable, if your dog comes in with head, ears and tail up, enthusiastic about joining you. Coming to you always should be positive and pleasurable because being with you feels safe to the dog. Your dog's coming always should be acknowledged.

Off-leash recall requires a good relationship between you and your dog.

You are not begging your dog to come, you are directing it to do so. But it should want to come to you.

When your dog reaches you, it should face you and assume a "sit." Always acknowledge its coming.

When you want your dog to come, by the way, it doesn't matter whether you say "Come," "Here, Boy," or "Burger and Fries." Your dog couldn't care less. Pick a command that's comfortable for you, and use it exclusively and consistently. What the words mean to your dog is whatever you teach him they mean.

At this stage of training, you should be in no hurry to take your dog off leash. First you'll use the six-foot leash, then the 25-foot line, gradually working farther away, increasing the distance only a few feet at a time, and achieving perfection at each distance before moving on to the next. Eventually you will stretch that line out on the ground, and walk beyond it to places from which you'll recall your dog. If the dog does not comply, you step forward, pick up the line and use it again to reel him in. Then reward him.

It is likely to take about three weeks to gain compliance in this if you're giving a lesson once a day. But this is a task with which you really must take your time. Jumping ahead will set up both you and the dog for failure.

If you have an imperfect relationship with the dog, you probably will not have much success with this until you fix the foundation of your relationship. And that doesn't happen in a day. It happens over a period of weeks, after you go back to the basics and re-instruct in fundamental training and reinforcement.

Off-Leash Heeling

The other new advanced-level skill is off-leash heeling. As with recall, if any little thing is wrong in your relationship with your dog, he will not heel for you off-leash. Your first prerequisite will be to fix the relationship.

Next, your dog must heel on-leash with close to 100 percent perfection before you can expect him to perform off-leash. An on-leash correction for him must be a rare event. He must have shown you through his behavior that he has an excellent grasp of the on-leash exercise.

Here, then, is how I proceed. I start with my dog sitting facing forward at my left side, its six-foot training leash attached to its training collar in the usual way. Normally, I would grip my end of the leash in my right hand, with the leash extending across the front of my body to the dog. For this exercise, however, I will drape the leash over the back of my neck, like a scarf, coming up over the front of my left shoulder, across the back of my neck, and extending down over the front of my right shoulder. The leash should hang loosely, providing the dog with the usual four to six inches of slack.

The leash will rest comfortably on my neck throughout the exercise unless I need to use it for a correction. If using a toy or a treat I will have it in my right hand close to my chest, where the dog can see it.

I will step forward on my left foot, and give my dog a verbal command to heel, just as I would if we were practicing regular on-leash heeling. I want this exercise to appear to the dog to be nearly identical to the way we usually perform it. We will walk the same pattern we customarily walk on-leash. We might start with counter-clockwise circles, for example, for the same reason we started with that pattern in his on-leash training; a circular pattern eliminates the necessity for abrupt turns, and by moving counter-clockwise with the dog on our left we have the ability to guide or herd the dog because he is on the inside of the circle. It would be more challenging if he were on the outside of the circle.

I walk with as natural a stride as possible. If the dog needs a correction, I grab the leash and administer one. Remember: My dog already has a very strong grasp of heeling on-leash, so we are going to practice this new method for a long while, until he masters it and needs very little or no correction. I will wait until he shows me he has a very good understanding of this before I take it to the next step.

When you begin this exercise with counter-clockwise circles, it is possible your dog may perform without an error. Eventually, after you are convinced he can perform nearly flawlessly, you will want to change the pattern of your walk. A logical next step might be to switch to clockwise circles. Here, it is very likely your dog will need a correction or two to remind him that he needs to turn with you and to maintain the pace. When your dog performs correctly for 12 to 20 paces, stop and reward him.

Eventually you no doubt will want to teach him to negotiate turns of 90 and 180 degrees. As with a beginning dog, you always should turn in the same direction while the dog masters this skill. You certainly will want to teach him how to turn both ways, but don't attempt to teach both at the same time. First master one, and then the other.

The mistake a new trainer usually makes, whether engaged in basic, intermediate or advanced training, is that he doesn't build a strong enough foundation before he moves forward. Remember, this isn't a race. Your dog's performance will be more reliable in the long run if you take your time building the foundation and don't rush through the instruction.

Light Line

When your dog is performing nearly flawlessly with the leash draped over your neck, and can circle left, circle right, turn corners and reverse direction, it is time to go to a light line. You can create such a line out of strong twine or clothesline. Use the lightest-weight material you can find that's strong enough to telegraph corrections without breaking. Approximately 6 to 12 inches is the right length, depending on the size of your dog. You don't want the line to drag on the ground and risk tripping the dog. Tie the line to the live ring on his training collar, the same ring to which you attach his leash, and let the line dangle from the collar.

Attach your leash to the same ring. After three minutes to five minutes of on-leash heeling, have the dog sit facing forward at your left side, and prepare to unhook the leash. If you are using a toy or a treat, the dog should be aware that you have it. Also, if he's a bright dog, he's going to be attuned to the sound of the clasp coming off his collar.

This is an important moment. If he's a normal dog, the sound of that clasp coming off will signify freedom. He may bolt at the sound, or simply forge forward. Even if he does neither, the sound may signify to him that he has no responsibility anymore to his handler. Like a businessman who removes his necktie at the end of the work day, he could think that he has gone off duty. You must be observant as a handler and try to read your dog correctly and try to figure out what kind of meaning the sound has for him.

If he tries to bolt or to forge ahead, use the light line to administer a correction. You have taken a significant step when your dog begins to realize that, even with the leash removed, he still is on duty.

Now you practice the heeling exercises that you did with the dog on-leash and with the leash draped over your neck. You proceed the same way, starting with counter-clockwise circles, and learning one exercise to perfection before taking on another. Start with the light line in your left hand. It will feel to the dog as though he still is wearing his leash, even though he heard it come off. Step off on your left foot. Take a few steps with line in hand and then, if your dog is doing well, drop the line nonchalantly, calling as little attention to the action as possible. Walk about 20 paces and then stop and reward your dog.

If you need to administer a correction, you grab the line and administer it with that.

The dog will show you by his behavior whether he is ready for this yet. If he is not, you must back up to an appropriate point in the training regimen, and bring him forward again, this time more slowly.

Eventually, if the dog's success permits it, you will work the exercises with no line at all. If you must administer a correction, you grab his collar to do so.

You can master all of this in your back yard, by the way, and then go down the street to the neighborhood park and discover that your dog fails miserably to perform the skills he seemed to handle so adeptly at home. Don't be mystified. You've got to master these skills in every location in which you want to use them. That means at the park, in the shopping center parking lot, at the street fair and in the office complex where you work. Remember the principle of cross-contextualization, which I discussed in Chapter 11.

Remember also that your role as trainer and your dog's role as trainee never end. Training a dog is not something you do one time. It is something you do throughout the lifetime of the dog. If you want your dog to have these skills throughout his life, you have to polish these skills throughout his life.

When, however, will you be at least temporarily done? How will you know when you've accomplished what you can reasonably expect to accomplish and have brought your dog to near the peak of his ability to perform?

You'll have achieved this goal when your dog can perform the tasks you've set before him with close to 100 percent reliability in the face of virtually any type of distraction that occurs. One-hundred percent reliability is not 100 percent if your dog can perform only in the absence of distractions. If you're down at the local park performing sit-stays and down-stays and off-leash heeling, and the dog does well only until the train rolls through town, you don't have 100 percent reliability.

A lot of amateur trainers instinctively work where they won't be bothered by distractions, because they know that if distractions occur, their dog's performance will suffer.

However, the opposite tack is needed. If the Amtrak comes through town at 2:52 p.m., I'm going to be down there by the tracks at 2:45 p.m. and starting to work.

Chapter 15

Other Available Equipment

A dog owns nothing, yet is seldom dissatisfied.

– Irish proverb

What sort of equipment do you need to train your dog properly? Essentially, all you need is a collar and a leash or a leash substitute. They permit you first to keep a dog under your control. Second, they allow you to transmit instructions to your dog and, third, to telegraph corrections to him if needed.

So far, I have talked about standard leashes, light lines and long lines. I also have talked about metal training collars, including how to fit and install them. Equipment, including collars, comes in many varieties, however, so let's talk about some of those and about the purposes for which they are designed.

Collars

Other kinds of collars besides metal training collars include leather, fabric or nylon slip collars or choke collars; leather or nylon flat collars, that buckle shut like a belt; Martingale collars, which are part fabric and part chain; prong or "pinch" collars and electronic collars. I'll discuss each of these.

A fabric or nylon slip collar usually consists of tubular nylon or fabric material with a metal ring on each end. It is used the same way as a chain collar, but is not as effective for teaching.

A nylon or leather flat collar is the type commonly seen on neighborhood dogs, and often contains a metal plate or an attached metal tag that provides the owner's name, address and phone number. It usually also sports licensing tags and tags that provide information about the dog's vaccination history, and sometimes a microchip number for identification. In terms of usefulness, a flat collar attached to a leash can keep a dog from leaving an area without permission, but it is of little value for training with leash corrections for most dogs.

A Martingale collar is a part-fabric and part-chain collar of which the

A Martingale collar is part fabric, part chain. The chain portion goes over the back of the dog's neck.

fabric portion encompasses the neck. It can administer a correction similar to but more moderate than one administered by a chain "choke" collar.

Prong collars are made of metal, with prongs that are rounded on the end and that protrude inward, toward the dog's neck. When used correctly, they pull the loose skin of the neck together and administer a pinch, the same type of correction that dogs administer to each other.

The electronic collar, also known as an e-collar, administers an electronic sensation, a vibration or an aerosol spray to correct a dog for a mistake.

Fitting and Using Collars

Let's talk a bit about how to use the various types of collars correctly. First, a dog should wear a training collar only during training sessions. An unsupervised animal can catch its collar on a variety of things, and may not be able to free itself. If it is wearing any type of training collar, it might become seriously injured. A better collar to leave on your dog when it is unsupervised is a leather or nylon flat collar, carrying proper identification.

To install a flat collar properly, unbuckle it, place it around your dog's neck, and buckle it so it is comfortably snug. The collar should not be so loose that your dog can back out of it. Since a dog's head usually is larger in circumference than its neck, a collar that is comfortably snug will prevent the animal from pulling his head through it.

A Martingale collar should be just large enough to slide over a dog's head, like a chain collar.

Prong collars usually don't come with directions, and people commonly use them incorrectly. Many people form them in a circle and slip them over the dog's head like a chain collar. But in that case, they are far too large for the dog. To put one on correctly, squeeze one of the prongs together to disassemble a link and open the collar. Put the collar around your dog's neck and fit it carefully to the circumference of the neck so it is comfortably snug, and then reassemble it on the dog. To fit it properly, you may have to take some links out or add some links.

If a dog is wearing a prong collar, it should wear it high up on the neck, just under the jaw and behind the ears, on the smallest part of his neck. The closer to the chest, the larger the circumference of the neck becomes. If the collar hangs too low, it is too large, and you must take one or more links out. You want the collar stay at the top of the neck, just loose enough so that you

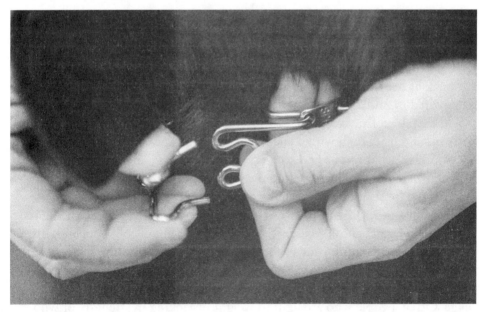

To fit a pinch collar properly, you may have to add or remove links.

To install collar, disengage a link, place collar around dog's neck, and reconnect the link.

can slide your fingers between the prongs and the dog's neck.

This collar's prongs are not sharp, but the collar works by grabbing loose skin of the dog's neck and simulating the nip that a mother administers to the neck of her puppy when correcting it. It's a kind of correction a canine is hard-wired to understand. You use the prong collar in the same manner you would a chain collar, except that the corrections you employ are administered with less intensity than with a chain collar to send the same message.

A prong collar can be an excellent tool when fitted and used correctly. When fitted and used incorrectly, however, it can become a weapon. If the collar is too loose, it doesn't have the ability to grab loose skin and simulate a gentle nip. Instead, it jams its prongs into the neck, possibly painfully.

Whether you choose to use a prong collar or a chain collar depends on several things, including your size and physical abilities and the size, strength and character of your dog. Dogs may be soft, medium or hard in character. A dog that is hard in character is one that may not shrink readily from a challenge. Often, people who are light in weight or lacking in strength, or who

Collar is fitted correctly when it is comfort- ably snug and you can insert your fingers between prongs and dog's neck.

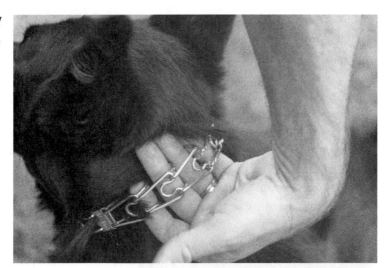

are elderly or disabled, find that a prong collar will help to enhance their ability to manage a large, hard-to-control dog.

However, psychological factors also can impact a decision about whether to use a prong collar. A dog that lacks confidence may not be a suitable candidate for such a collar, nor would one that already is sensitive to correction. Also, any dog that does not understand your leadership role is unsuitable. For example, a large, strongly assertive Rottweiler that you have not worked with may not be a good candidate, because he may object to being corrected by you in the manner that a parent corrects a puppy. You've got to start with a dog that is willing to acknowledge your leadership. Then, even a generally assertive

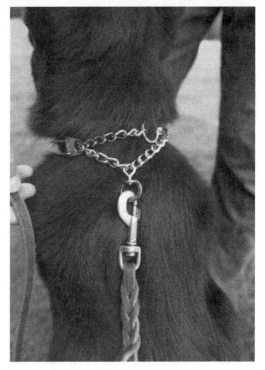

Attach leash to loop provided on the prong collar, which should be on the back of the dog's neck.

dog such as a Rottweiler could be an appropriate candidate. If my relation-ship with the Rottweiler were far enough along that he acknowledged my leadership, I could certainly put him in a prong collar on day one, although it's important to remember that just because this individual is a member of an assertive breed doesn't necessarily mean that he needs a prong collar.

How about electronic collars, sometimes called "shock" collars? Are they cruel? Reasonable people can differ about that. A lot depends on how they are used. Any training tool used incorrectly can be cruel, and if you plan to use an electronic collar, you must do it right. It is always a good idea to consult with a professional before deciding to use an electronic collar, and if in a profes-sional's opinion its use is appropriate, to seek guidance from that professional on how best to go about it.

Once a decision is made to proceed, the electronic collar goes on with a buckle or clasp, and you place it so that its two electronic probes are high on the neck under the dog's chin, comfortably snug against his throat. The collar produces a brief electronic stimulation when it is triggered either manually by the handler or automatically by the dog's behavior. You can adjust the strength of the stimulation, and should set it at the lowest possible level that achieves an appropriate response from the dog. In no event should you set the correc-tion at a higher level than you are willing to tolerate in the palm of your hand.

One of the three things for which trainers most commonly use electron-ic collars is to correct excessive, repetitive, nonsense barking. A second is to administer a correction when the dog is off leash and away from you, such as in gun-dog training for pointing and retrieving breeds. A third is to establish an invisible-fence boundary.

Occasionally, extreme cases come to training facilities for behavioral rehabilitation in which a tool like the electronic collar can be effective. Let me give you a worst-case scenario. A dog comes into a facility for treatment of a behavioral problem. The dog is nervous, pacing, barking and howling. Its problem may be extreme anxiety. In the process of frantically pacing and bark-ing, the dog works itself into a psychological condition in which it is oblivious to its environment. Its heart and respiration rates go through the ceiling, its mind reaches a frantic, unhealthy state, and the dog passes the point where it is able to calm itself. Its behavior now can become so frantic that it can hurt itself, perhaps by chewing on a steel kennel door and risking breaking its teeth and cutting its gums, or by chewing on its own body. Attempts to calm it with voice or the touch of a hand do not reach its brain.

To see something like this is tremendously saddening, and not to intercept the behavior and bring the dog some peace is cruel.

This may be an appropriate situation for an electronic collar at a low-level setting. If the collar is a bark monitor, as opposed to a remote-training collar, the dog's whines, cries or barks will elicit light transmissions to interrupt his thought process. Most dogs learn within minutes that they are in charge of the strap and the pulses it emits. They discover that they can stop the stimulation instantly by stopping their rant. The magic here is that as the dog desists from the behavior, his

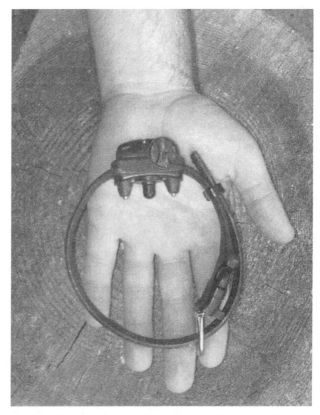

E-collar should be comfortably snug, with prongs high on the dog's neck under its jaw. (Photo by Dianna M. Young)

brain begins to calm and his body follows suit. His heart rate and respiration return to normal, and in a few minutes he likely will lie quietly down on his bed.

I believe it is humane to be able to offer that gift to him. It certainly is preferable to some other possible alternatives, such as sedating him. Sedating tends to mask a problem, and only temporarily. An unsedated dog can address the problem. Once his brain calms, he can experience his environment in a positive way and develop a new opinion about it.

Speaking of sedation, do you know how many dogs in the USA are heavily medicated every Fourth of July? Thousands. They're sedated because they've never been socialized properly to the sound of fireworks, and in many cases the unaccustomed noise makes them frantic. Once that fear process begins, the behavior can feed on itself and become more and more out of control. Since a dog may not always be able to avoid fireworks, it is good if he can learn to live with them if possible. An electronic bark monitor can intercept the behaviors that are symptomatic of the dog's frenzy and, because he no longer can perform the behaviors, he often will lie down and begin to relax. Depending on the severity of his behavior, this might help, but not necessarily in all cases.

An inexperienced observer might ask whether it is appropriate to punish a dog for being afraid. That question itself would reveal the questioner's lack of understanding. Of course it is not appropriate to punish for fear. An electronic collar never should be used as punishment, no matter what the behavior. In this case, however, the owner is not aiming to punish the dog, but to calm it.

How about an electronic collar that is activated manually by a handler during training sessions? I prefer to use a leash and collar to send messages to my dog whenever possible, because it makes the relationship between us personal. But if I'm working with a hunting dog or a service dog or with any other dog that is a football field's length away and I don't have an opportunity to communicate personally, electronics might be appropriate.

Another situation in which electronics can be useful is in discouraging an outdoor dog from crossing the boundaries of its owner's unfenced property. A specially adapted electronic collar is properly affixed to a dog that has been trained to recognize boundaries, is set at the lowest current level that will get the dog's attention, and the dog is turned loose in the yard. The yard is surrounded by a wire or other triggering mechanism that will activate the collar's stimulation if the dog approaches too closely. In cases where vehicle traffic races by outside the yard, the collar literally can save a life.

Some electronic collars provide a vibrator option. Instead of feeling an electronic stimulation, a dog feels its collar vibrate, the same way you may feel your cell phone vibrate in your pocket. This collar mode is appropriate and effective with dogs that are naturally sensitive to correction.

A word of warning, though: If you're thinking about using an electronic collar, I recommend you get professional guidance before doing so. You can send an incorrect message to your dog with such a collar, and you may end up compounding a problem instead of solving it. Electronic collars can be very effective for certain kinds of issues and for certain kinds of dogs, but not for others. Professional coaching is a good idea.

Let me tell you about a novice handler I happened to observe one time who decided to use electronic stimulation to get his dog to conform to his wishes. In the process, he stacked mistakes on top of other mistakes. First, he hadn't had any professional coaching in use of the collar. He planned to wing it. Next, he was working with a dog with which he didn't have any dependable recall. Third, the dog was off-leash. Fourth, he set the collar's stimulation level too high. Eventually, the time came when this handler thought it would be a good idea to administer a correction. It wasn't. He had administered it at the wrong time and at too high a level, and the dog turned inside-out with surprise. The animal didn't know what had just happened – or why – and he lit out for the high country so it wouldn't happen again. The handler couldn't stop him, and it was a couple of days before he saw his dog again.

Under the proper circumstances, however, and with an appropriate dog, a trainer can use an electronic collar to eliminate problems that might not be addressable any other way. Let me tell you about an experience I had with one of my own dogs. She was a beautiful German shepherd dog whose name was Inga. I had installed a new automatic sprinkler system in my yard. Inga had free run of the yard at times, and when a sprinkler head popped up and the water came on, Inga would go for it. Her natural prey drive was more than she could resist, and she loved to grab those spewing plastic sprinkler heads and chew them up. If I was in the yard when Inga went for one, I'd administer a correction, and she would abort her mission. But when I wasn't there to correct her, she continued to attack sprinklers.

I was replacing sprinkler heads weekly, if not daily, and couldn't afford to continue. So, I put an electronic collar on Inga, at a setting I knew wouldn't alarm her, and took the manual triggering device into the house to an upstairs window overlooking the yard. The sprinklers came on, and she pounced on one. The moment she got her mouth around it, I tapped the button on my device and administered a stimulation. Her reaction was immediate. She jumped backward a step and looked over her right shoulder, and then over her left shoulder, apparently thinking, *What the heck was that?* Then she walked away from the sprinkler.

Inga couldn't see me through the window, and a few minutes later, temptation got the better of her again. Inga went for a different sprinkler head, and I tapped the button again. It stopped her in her tracks. A few more minutes, and Inga gave it a third try, with the same result.

That was all it took. In three repetitions, Inga learned not to attack the sprinkler heads, and she never bothered one again. The beauty of it was that she equated the correction with her behavior, and not with her handler. So, going forward, it didn't matter if I was in the yard or not. She believed that if she attacked a sprinkler head, God would tap her on the shoulder.

Thinking Creatively About Equipment

You also can carry out remote corrections, by the way, with equipment other than electronics. Let me tell you the story of Jago, a tremendously large, tremendously friendly male German shepherd dog I owned years ago. I had moved into a small rental house that didn't have any enclosed place in the kitchen in which to place a container for garbage. So my garbage container, a plastic receptacle with a swinging lid, sat out on the kitchen floor. When Jago pushed aside the lid and stuck his snout into the container, I reprimanded him. Being a highly intelligent dog, he quickly learned that this is an activity that you don't do when your leader is at home.

But sometimes the leader is not at home. I had to go to work at a nearby dog-training center every day, and Jago had the run of the house on days that he didn't go with me. Sometimes I'd come home and find the container accidentally knocked over and garbage lying about the kitchen floor because Jago had stuck his head into the container and gotten his head caught in the lid, upsetting everything. Although Jago was a smart dog, he hadn't figured out how to sweep up the mess, so the evidence of his behavior would be there on the floor when I got home.

Was Jago a bad dog? Not at all. He was just a dog. And one of the characteristics of dogs is that they live in the moment. Poor Jago wasn't able to get his head around the fact that I'd be home in a few hours, and if he got into the garbage now, I would discover it later, when I got there. He simply knew he could do it now without risk. I had to devise a plan therefore, to create a correction that appeared to be related directly to that activity and not to depend on my presence.

I let the garbage get high enough in the can to be within reach of his snout when he pushed aside the swinging lid. Then I set a mouse trap on top of the garbage, loaded its spring, and placed a paper plate on top of the trap. The plate was to protect the dog, and the trap was so small it was incapable of catching Jago's large snout even without the plate. I went out the door, and crept around to a window where I could peek past the edge of the curtain and see what happened in the kitchen.

I hardly had gotten out of the house when Jago went right for the garbage container. He pushed the swinging lid aside, stuck his snout down into the garbage, and, Pow! The trap went off with a loud snap under the plate, startling the unsuspecting dog. He took off at top speed across the slippery linoleum floor, performing some splits as he rounded the corner on his way out of the kitchen. I had to repeat the lesson only once, and my problem was solved. Jago had concluded that the garbage would get him if he stuck his snout into it.

Harnesses

This chapter wouldn't be complete without a word about harnesses. More and more people seem to be using them in place of collars.

Harnesses come in several types, and we will talk about two main types. The first is a standard harness, the other is a no-pull harness.

With a standard harness, the leash hooks on top of the dog's back, sometimes near the shoulders, where the harness crosses the dog's spine.

With a no-pull harness, the leash usually clips to the chest area. This harness is designed to make it difficult or uncomfortable for the dog to pull. It is important to know that a no-pull harness does not teach a dog *not* to pull, it only makes the dog uncomfortable when doing so. Therefore, a dog often chooses not to pull while wearing one.

Often people use regular harnesses on large dogs that are not properly trained. The result is predictable. At one of my dog-boarding businesses, harnesses have become very popular among the clientele. Not so coincidentally, many of the clients express the same complaint about their dogs. "The dog is dragging me all over the place," they say.

I reply, "Yeah, well, have you ever watched the Iditarod?

Around our neck of the woods, most dog people are familiar with that annual televised sled-dog race from Anchorage to Nome. The dogs in that race all wear harnesses.

My point is that most harnesses are designed for pulling. They're not effective as a teaching device, and they're especially not effective if you're trying to break your dog of pulling on its leash during walks. If you're using a harness and you're complaining you're being pulled, be aware that you're using a device that's designed to encourage it.

Chapter 16

The Effects of Environment

If it's true that dogs don't go to heaven, I want to go where they go.
— Will Rogers (1879 – 1935)

In an earlier chapter, I talked about canine temperament, which is genetic. Temperament is implanted at birth, although it might be modified to some extent later by environment. Your dog is born essentially with the temperament he has, and it plays a pivotal role in his behavior.

The other pivotal thing that contributes to your dog's behavior is, of course, his environment. And you are a major part of that environment. What you do has tremendous impact on the kind of dog he becomes.

Unfortunately, your impact sometimes can be negative. Many dogs exhibit owner-caused behavioral problems, the most common of which, in descending order, are anxiety, aggression and destructive behavior. These are not the only possibilities, however. An owner-induced problem can be just about anything imaginable. Some owners like to brush off a problem with the claim that they just "have a bad dog." The fact is, however, that whether a sound dog is well behaved or poorly behaved is a reflection on the owner.

For example: I leave my dog alone in the car, and he chews up the upholstery while I'm shopping. Is he a bad dog? Or am I a neglectful owner, because I allowed a dog with anxiety issues to be left in my car unattended?

Another example: I put my dog outside in our fenced yard, and when I check on him I find he has dug holes in the lawn, pulled landscaping plants out of the ground and chewed some siding off the house. Bad dog? Or bored dog, because I left him unsupervised in the yard for too long with no constructive way to entertain himself?

The questions can be painful, because they force us to take a hard look in the mirror.

How, then, can you avoid owner-induced behavioral problems? The answer is simple; by training your dog properly.

Anthropomorphism

Probably the single most important factor working against effective training is a phenomenon known as "anthropomorphism." That's a 24-dollar word with Greek roots that means the attribution of human characteristics to non-human things, such as inanimate objects, gods or animals. A lot of us attribute human characteristics to nature, for example. Those characteristics may be either evil or benign, even though we know that Mother Nature is neither of those things but rather is completely impersonal. We do the same thing with animals, and all of us are guilty of it to some degree.

You may know people who carry on one-way conversations with their dogs, for example, and lots of people carry their dogs' photos around on their cell phones, along with those of their kids and grandchildren. According to one survey, nearly half of American dog owners celebrate their dogs' birthdays. Cute? Well, maybe.

But anthropomorphism also has an ugly side. It rears its head when we decide to punish a dog for ignoring a concept that he has no ability to grasp. For example, Joe Dogowner is headed out the door for work. "See you in about 10 hours, Jake," he calls to his dog. "Don't touch that leftover birthday cake!"

Ten hours later, Joe returns and discovers that Jake ate the cake in spite of the warning. So poor Jake gets his hind end whipped or gets banished to the garage or tied to a tree in the back yard. Maybe he doesn't get fed that evening, because Joe wants "to teach him a lesson."

Unfortunately, the lesson is lost on poor Jake. In the first place, Jake doesn't speak English, so the warning meant nothing to him. In the second place, by the time Joe got home Jake had forgotten about the cake. Dogs live in the moment, not in the future or in the past, and so Jake had no idea what the punishment was about.

I run into these situations all the time, and they make me tremendously sad. I know that anthropomorphism has kicked in when I hear Joe complaining about how Jake "knew he had been bad. He knew when I got home he was going to get it, and when I came in and saw that the cake was gone, Jake was cowering on the floor with his ears laid back and a guilty look on his face."

I guess it never occurred to Joe that Jake was cowering not because of the cake, but because his owner had gone into a rant, and it made Jake afraid even though he didn't know what the rant was about.

So how do you deal with anthropomorphism? You deal with it by learning how a dog's mind operates. Dogs learn through repetition. They cannot think deductively or anticipate probable outcomes from an array of possibilities. They cannot look ahead or reminisce. They cannot worry about what you might do five hours from now when you discover their misbehavior of this moment, because they cannot wrap their heads around such a concept. In this respect their brains are radically different from ours. A young dog is *not* a fuzzy child, and so the way we respond to a particular situation with our dog must be different than it would be if we were dealing with another person.

Anxiety

Sometimes, our behavior as a leader and teacher must be almost counter-intuitive. For example, it is normal for a dog to be unsure in certain situations, and common for us to see a fear response from time to time. But what we do with our dog when that occurs is critical, and the correct response may surprise you. I often see owners try to console a dog that is anxious. That's a normal human instinct and it probably works fine with a child, but it's a mistake with a dog because it amounts to praising the animal for its nervous reaction. If we see undesirable behavior from our dog, even if such behavior is fear-induced, we need to interrupt that behavior, not reinforce it.

For example, our dog Jake is at the veterinarian's office, and he doesn't want to be there. That's a fairly typical canine reaction to the situation. But maybe Jake's anxiety is causing him to behave aggressively toward the veterinarian and her staff. He lies on the examination table and growls softly whenever anyone approaches. His owner stands beside him, trying to calm him. As Jake growls, his owner strokes him, saying, "It's okay, Jake, it's okay. The doctor won't hurt you."

Keep in mind that Jake doesn't understand English, so what this sounds like to Jake is, "Good job, Jake, good job. Rip her face off."

As far as Jake is concerned, he's getting praise for aggressive behavior. So Jake growls louder. And Jake's owner has no idea the role that he is playing in the behavior.

What the owner needs to do is to interrupt Jake's undesirable behavior, not encourage it. Sometimes a correction with the training collar can make it clear to Jake that his behavior not only is unacceptable, but that it will not be tolerated.

The interruption is required even if Jake is not showing aggression but is exhibiting only anxiety, and this is what a human may find counter-intuitive. When you praise and encourage an anxious dog, you are praising cowering, trembling and fear. If that is not the behavior you want, you need to interrupt it, just as you would interrupt any other undesirable behavior, because that with which you do not actively disagree you silently endorse.

Do you know what a pack of dogs does with a frightened and nervous dog in its midst? They correct it by nipping and biting, and sometimes they can get rough. Dogs know instinctively how to fix the problem, and we should accord them some respect for understanding their own make-up. While it might seem to us that a dog correcting another dog for fright might add to its fear, interrupting its nervous behavior often puts it in a frame of mind that allows calmness to begin to return. When it feels weak and vulnerable, a dog longs for a strong and competent leader to which it can hand off all of its worries. The person who coos and clucks over his dog comes across to the dog as weak and vulnerable himself. That's the opposite of strong and competent.

Always remember, however: The solution to problematic behavior has two parts. First, you interrupt the dog's undesirable behavior. Second, you step up and take over all of the issues that were causing your dog anxiety. How does this work in real life? It works by you taking on more responsibility.

Taking Responsibility

In my training programs, I often bring my four-pound Mexican Chihuahua into classes that contain what some people think of as bully breeds – Rottweilers, pit bulls, American bulldogs and so forth. I do so because she has a tremendously calming influence on other dogs. Peanut always walks into class on leash and on her own four feet, brimming with good-natured self-confidence. Often, when she arrives for her first class, one of the bullies will try to intimidate her by growling or even trying to rush across the room to accost her. This doesn't faze her. Usually, she'll ignore the aggressive dog, which might be lunging at the end of its leash while its owner tries to control it. Peanut just goes about her business, refusing to engage, and projecting a calmness that eventually becomes infectious.

New students in my classes often express amazement at this. "My good-

ness," they sometimes say, "doesn't that little dog realize how much danger she's in? Doesn't she know that this Rottweiler could snap her in half? Why isn't she afraid?"

My response is, "She's not afraid because, in all the years she has been with me, I have never put her in a position where she had to deal with conflict. She has learned through repetition thousands of times over that if there is ever a problem, I'm right on top of it. I'm always aware of what is going on around us, and if that Rottie made a dash for her, he would have to go through me to get to her. It has never occurred to Peanut that she might have to protect herself from a Rottweiler. As far as she is concerned, I can stop speeding cars and speeding bullets, not to mention speeding Rottweilers."

That is the kind of comfort that canines find in strong leadership. And that is the kind of leadership you must provide.

This is an extremely important concept in developing the proper relationship between you and your dog. It calls for constant vigilance on your part, combined with proactive behavior, so let's explore it a little further. A good example of what commonly happens nearly occurred one day while my husband, Jason, was teaching a class in basic obedience in a supermarket parking lot. He had taken the class of about a dozen people and their dogs to the lot to introduce some distractions into the training scenario, because any well-trained dog needs to be able to function in a disciplined way even in the presence of distractions.

Midway through the lesson, Jason spotted a woman across the parking lot about a football field away, locked on his little group like enemy radar and moving in their direction at warp speed.

As he continued to lecture and to demonstrate dog-handling techniques, Jason kept one eye on the woman, who was closing fast. When she neared his group, Jason noticed that she was focused on one particular animal, a beautiful German shepherd dog of exceptionally hard character that was working with its handler on exercises. The handler, a very capable person, had her back to the approaching woman.

As the intruder hurried closer, Jason noted that she stared intently at the dog. The handler still was not aware of her approach, but the handler's dog by now was staring back at the woman with an intensity that equaled her own.

Apparently, the well-intentioned woman was responding to an urge to pet this beautiful animal. The dog was getting ready to respond to an urge of its own.

Just before the woman reached the dog, Jason stepped forward and placed himself between them.

"Whoa, whoa!" he told the woman. "He's the wrong dog for that!"

At this point the handler realized what had been about to happen, and jumped into the conversation.

"He doesn't do well with people coming at him head-on," she told the woman.

The woman stopped. Perhaps embarrassed now by Jason's and the handler's reactions, she turned to walk away, but paused to toss an angry comment. "That dog must not be very well socialized!" she said.

Actually, the dog was quite well socialized. It just didn't have a personality that permitted it to enjoy a friendly mauling by a stranger. And rather than criticizing the dog or its training, the woman might have considered thanking Jason and the handler for keeping her from getting bitten.

In fact, if Jason or the dog's handler had not intervened, that's probably what would have happened.

The incident provided Jason with some excellent lessons to share with his class. The first lesson was, if you feel the inexplicable urge to fondle a strange dog, never approach it without permission from its handler. Even with permission, approach indirectly to avoid causing the animal to think that you might be a threat.

Lesson number two was, if you are a handler and someone approaches your dog with the intention of touching it, there is nothing the matter with stepping between that person and the dog and informing the person politely that the dog doesn't like to be handled by strangers.

Look at it this way: Would you allow a stranger to rush up to your child and fondle the child's face or run fingers through your child's hair? Would you allow a stranger to do the same to you? Why, then, would you allow someone to do that to your dog?

This meeting-a-stranger scenario can be critical to you and your dog because if you don't handle it correctly it can undermine your whole relationship.

Virtually all strangers who approach are well-intentioned, and many handlers see no harm in allowing the scenario to play out. But that may not be the way your dog sees it. I was in a public venue a few years ago with a client who simply could not comprehend what was such a big deal about a stranger coming up and petting her somewhat uncomfortable dog.

"I'll show you what I'm talking about," I told her.

I left the client and walked halfway across the shopping center parking lot, then turned and caught her eye. I was about to do a little role-playing. Focused intently on her, I walked toward her at a rapid pace, never taking my eyes from hers. Still staring hard, I walked directly up to her and into her space, and then reached out and touched her face.

I could see her recoil.

"Now picture that if I were a stranger," I told her.

"Oh, my goodness!" she said. "That was creepy! If that really happened to me I'd be reaching for my can of Mace!"

Stopping Bullets

To boil this down to its essence, your dog needs to be able to count on its leader in encounters with strangers. If you stand back and let strangers accost him, you are not being a leader. And in the absence of a leader, your dog will assume the position by default. He has no choice; the behavior is encoded in his doggy DNA. If he – not you – is the pack leader, this will make itself felt in all aspects of your relationship.

You can avoid all the problems associated with this by stepping up to your leadership responsibility.

Let me tell you about the experience of one of my clients recently on Alki Beach in Seattle, where we were working with her pup. The day was sunny, and a lot of walkers, joggers, skateboarders and bicyclists were enjoying the area. My client's puppy was a magnet for passers-by, many of whom wanted to man-handle it in a friendly manner. My client allowed anyone to do so. The puppy tolerated it, but I could see anxiety build up in the pup every time a person approached. My client didn't understand where the anxiety was coming from. I explained it to her, and told her what we needed to do about it.

A minute later, a couple came down the street toward us. The man was fairly large, six-three or six-four and impressively built. The woman was pretty big herself, and together they were quite imposing. As they approached they spotted the pup. I could see their eyes light up, and they made a course correction that would bring them to a spot where they would block our path.

This time, however, my client stepped between them and her dog, put her hand out, and very nicely explained, "My pup is in training. I appreciate your intent, and thank you so much, but it would be better if you didn't pet her."

The pup of course understood none of the conversation, but it watched what her owner had done. My client was a petite woman, and next to this imposing couple she looked tiny. Yet she had stepped forward, put up her hand and – in her puppy's eyes – had stopped a speeding bullet. The look on the pup's face was priceless.

In the hour that we worked together that day, my client stopped about eight speeding bullets. With each repetition the puppy became more and more self-assured. With every new encounter, the pup looked to its owner expectantly, and by the eighth repetition we could see that the pup was confident that the next stranger would be stopped.

Some dogs actually like the attention of strangers. A lot of dogs don't, but will tolerate it. Some dogs, like the German shepherd dog in Jason's class, won't even tolerate it.

You can relieve your dog of a lot of anxiety by following the example of my Seattle client. By intervening with people who approach uninvited, you demonstrate to your dog that you are in charge of pack security. Not only does that lift a lot of stress from your dog, it sends an important message to your dog as well. The message is that you clearly are its leader, because in the canine world, the job of pack security always is reserved for the pack leader.

Spoiling

I can't tell you the number of new people who come into our boarding facility to drop off their dogs and proceed to tell us how thoroughly they have spoiled the dog. I think in many cases they consider this our orientation to their dog and to them, and they often speak with pride about how badly their dog is spoiled. They seem to regard it as evidence that they're great guys who really, really love their dogs.

I don't see it that way, exactly. Webster's New Compact Dictionary for School and Office says that "to spoil" is to impair, damage or harm the character or nature of something by excessive indulgence. Since when is impairing, damaging or harming your dog evidence of love?

In extreme cases of spoiling, I've seen people actually killing their dogs with kindness. A common example is a dog that is morbidly obese. You know that he's not feeding himself. Yet here he is, often with diabetes or congestive heart failure or joint injuries or even broken bones frequently related to his excessive weight. I have seen obese dogs that have had to be euthanized before their time for these or similar reasons, shortening the time they get to spend with the person who claims to love them so much.

Overindulgence with food is immediately apparent. Other forms of overindulgence may be less obvious, and may impair, damage or harm not the dog's body, but its behavior. We have clients, for example, who overindulge their dogs with love and praise or with activities and events that their dogs like. Is love a bad thing? Of course not. People want to love and praise their dogs and to let them participate in events they enjoy, but responsible leadership is all about balance and timing. And overindulgence is not so much about loving a dog too much as it is loving it at inappropriate times.

Sometimes I notice that people who come in for a behavior assessment or a private training lesson will keep one hand on the leash and use the other hand to stroke their dog in excessive repetitions as they talk with me. Sometimes, the dog may be over-excited and it's getting praise, may be nervous and it's getting praise or may be aggressive and it's getting praise. Or, it may just happen to be breathing, and it's getting praise for that.

Praise for a job well done is one of the resources you can use to reinforce good behavior. If you hand it out willy-nilly, your dog has no motivation to work for you or to behave appropriately for you. It's all about balance. You should not withhold good things from your dog. But you should dole them out at appropriate times, using them to improve your relationship. If your dog wants for nothing, he needs you for nothing, and you'll find in training that he has nothing to offer you, not even basic respect.

When you overindulge with love and praise, you produce a dog that is unmotivated to work for you, that lacks respect for you and that, usually, is very demanding. You can rest assured that he wasn't born that way. A dog like that has been taught to be that way.

Teens

In some respects, dealing with a young dog is somewhat like dealing with kids. They're cute and cuddly for a while and then, all of a sudden, they begin to approach sexual maturity and often transform into stubborn, poorly behaved individuals. This happens with dogs about six to eight months of age, and the behavioral changes are similar in males and females. How long can you expect this poor behavior continue? Indefinitely, if you don't correct it. The behavior will continue until you reel the dog in.

As new clients begin our training programs, we stress the importance of keeping their untrained or only partially trained dogs on leashes, both indoors and out, so they have a way to communicate effectively with their pets. Often, the owner of a pup will reply, "I don't need a leash, because my puppy follows me everywhere I go." The person and the pup are like a momma duck and a duckling, with the little one waddling after Momma as though it's tied to her tail feathers. Some clients think this is going to last forever. I tell them it will change.

Between about six and eight months of age, the pup will start to become more independent and more confident. He will become less dependent on his owner. He will develop more and more curiosity about the world, and eventually will begin to explore it on his own, to the extent that he is able. This is normal behavior.

At this point, you should attach the pup to a short leash or light line and let him haul it around the house. It gives you something to grab in order to communicate with him.

Here's something to think about: Did you know that a great number of the dogs you can find in an animal shelter are roughly 12 to 18 months of age? In other words, they're in the midst of their adolescence. What this implies is that for the first six or eight months of life, this dog probably was adorable, agreeable and compliant and lived in a loving home. Then it became a teen, and it was not so much any of those things anymore. By the time it hit 12 to 18 months, its human family apparently was at its wit's end. This is an age at which an untrained dog really can start to lose its charm, and its owner can become exasperated enough to surrender it to a shelter.

So take heed of what the shelter data are trying to tell you. If you expect to have a well-mannered adult dog, you need to begin shaping that dog early. It's not going to be an adorable little puppy forever, and so you have got to be standing by with training at the ready. Every puppy eventually becomes an adolescent, and if you haven't laid the proper foundation for it with discipline and structure, you have contributed to the problems that are almost sure to follow.

Setting the Bar

Lots of people set the bar for their dogs much too low. I don't know of many who set it too high. People often are satisfied if their dog meets just three low standards; that it doesn't defecate in the house (at least not very often), that it doesn't bite people (at least not very seriously) and that it doesn't wreck stuff (at least not most of the time). Some people believe that's as good as it gets.

They're wrong, of course. Dogs have much more to offer. But you have to expect good behavior from them and require it. You have to set the bar high. Every household has its own standards of pet behavior, so there are no clear rules that apply to every family and all of its pets. But whatever the rules are in your house, you should establish them, not your dog.

A lot of dog owners routinely deal with bad canine behavior by avoiding situations that provoke it. "My dog doesn't like strangers, so I don't introduce him to strangers." "My dog goes crazy when he sees other dogs, so I make sure he doesn't see other dogs." Setting the bar that low short-changes you in terms of the relationship that you could have – but don't have – with your pet. The choice is yours. You can have an ill-behaved dog that you put up with for 14 years, or you can have a rewarding 14-year relationship with a great companion.

Precisely where the bar is set will be different for every person and every dog. Some breeds of dog are highly intelligent and thrive on having work and purpose in their lives. Others are not as talented and may find training more of a challenge. If you are unclear about the potential of your dog, you might consult with a professional for advice on where to set the bar.

But remember this: It is not cruel to expect a high standard of behavior. Quite the opposite. In households with low expectations, I usually see frustrated, under-stimulated, anxiety-ridden dogs. They would improve in the face of a challenge. As human beings, we seek purpose in life. We want to feel that what we do is meaningful. Our dogs also do much better with discipline and purpose in their lives.

Chapter 17

Problem-Solving

We could have bought a small yacht with what we spent on our dog and all the things he destroyed. Then again, how many yachts wait by the door all day for your return?

– John Grogan (Marley and Me, 2005)

I talked with a client recently who was concerned that her pup continued to urinate and defecate in the house every few days at a point in his life by which he should have learned to do that outdoors. Almost all puppies have bowel and bladder control after 16 weeks, and certainly by 20 weeks. And this pup was 10 months old. So, what was going on?

I figured out the answer by questioning the client extensively about her and her husband's typical interactions with their dog.

It turns out, the pup had been doing fairly well with his house training – although not perfectly well – and because of his progress the owners had jumped ahead and given him free run of the house before he had achieved perfection. He'd been on a roll with his progress, they thought, and those occasional mistakes probably would disappear soon. But they didn't.

Every two or three days, when the pup was feeling lazy or his owners weren't tuned in to where he was and what he was up to, he'd leave them another gift in a hallway or a bedroom.

The cause of the problem here was that the owners hadn't built a strong behavioral foundation before they gave their pup its freedom. When they decided that the puppy was doing well enough, they stopped keeping an eye on him and forgot about the "two Cs" of housebreaking, which are crating or constant supervision.

By the time they came to see me, they thought they owned a bad dog. Actually, they owned a dog that was as consistent in going to the bathroom outdoors as they were in seeing to it that it happened. His behavior was a direct reflection of their own ineffectiveness.

I explained to them that they needed to go back to basics. Even though their pup was only 10 months old, it looked a lot like an adult dog, and so they thought of him in that way. What they needed to do, however, was to think of him as an eight-week-old puppy, and to treat him as such with crating or constant supervision, along with frequent trips outdoors on the leash. They had to rebuild his toilet-training foundation all over again, from the ground up, which would set him up for a success rate of nearly 100 percent.

Incomplete training and poor supervision are not always the issues with housebreaking failures, however. I worked with another client whose 15-month-old dog suddenly, and for no reason obvious to the owner, began to urinate on dog beds that were scattered about the house. The owner wondered if this was a housebreaking issue. But it turned out to be a bit more than that.

Although it sounded like a behavioral problem, I suggested to her that we ask a veterinarian to run a test on the dog's urine just to rule out the possibility of a urinary tract infection. She agreed to do that, and the test unexpectedly came back positive. What appeared to have been a behavioral issue actually had been caused by a physical ailment. When the infection was cured with antibiotics, so was the problem.

So, what is the most important take-away from these stories? It is this: For most canine behavioral problems, you can benefit greatly from professional input. Very often, a professional trainer or canine behaviorist – or, in some cases, a veterinarian – can provide you in one consultation with an accurate analysis of a problem's causes, and can lay out a program to correct it.

People who try to diagnose their own problems will approach them 99 times out of 100 from a human point of view, and that often will set up the diagnosis for error. If the person trying to help these dogs had misdiagnosed the reasons they were urinating or defecating indoors, the rehabilitation would have failed.

Bad bathroom habits are only one of many common behavioral problems that people bring to us in search of solutions, however. Let's talk about some of the others.

Aggression

Let me tell you about a client of mine who had a little dog that was a holy terror on the end of a leash. This diminutive guy threatened aggression against almost every dog he encountered while he was out on walks with his owner, and sometimes did the same even with people, lunging and snarling and carrying on. The behavior was a significant problem for the owner. Fortunately, the dog's relatively small size allowed his owner to prevent him from injuring others, but she found it both stressful and embarrassing to have to haul him in like an anchor every time he initiated yet another confrontation.

This was no pup who still was learning his manners, either. The dog was seven years old, and had behaved this way all of his life, and my client logically concluded that he must have been hard-wired at birth for aggressive behavior. She assumed, therefore, that nobody could do anything about it, and so she just tried to live with the problem. Finally, however, she ran out of patience and, while she didn't believe the problem really could be fixed, a part of her wanted to try. So she brought the dog to us, and asked if we could fix it.

It's good that she did. Because in the first few days he was with us, we discovered that this little fellow was not aggressive at all toward dogs or people. In fact, he was an incredibly social little guy. We discovered that the root of the problem was that the dog had felt tremendously vulnerable when tethered to the opposite end of a leash from the woman who owned him. She was a laid-back, non-assertive kind of a person, which disturbed her dog. Some people are like that, and it's certainly not a character defect. It's simply a personality trait, and a common one at that, which inclines a person to avoid behavior that might be considered confrontational. She broadcast this mindset clearly through her body language. I'm sure you know what I'm talking about. If a bad guy were hiding in a parking garage, this is the person he'd be waiting for, and he'd know her when he saw her. As a result, the little dog thought of himself in her company as live bait staked out on the end of a tether, waiting for some predator to come along and gobble him up.

We found that when he was on a leash with any of our staff – all experienced handlers – he was 10 feet tall and brimming with friendly confidence. On a leash with his owner, however, his attempted attacks on others were preemptive, driven by his anxiety about his own safety.

To eliminate the problem, what we needed to fix was not the dog. We needed to fix his owner.

It's a very common situation, and we have encountered it literally hundreds of times over the years. Not everyone is equipped by genetics or by training to broadcast confidence and assertiveness through their body language, and opening a discussion about it with such a person can be like venturing into a minefield. At Camano Island Kennels, however, we have successfully coached many people in the art of assertive body language to enhance their relationships with their dogs, and this woman was open to the idea.

She had been thrilled when she came to retrieve her dog from us. As far as she was concerned, we had performed a miracle. She had met a new dog in her own dog, one that she never had known before. When we explained the reason for the apparent change, she wanted to get on board with things that she could do to make the transition permanent.

We don't know the end of the story yet, because the dog went home with her only recently. But the last we saw of them, they were doing well together. Our hope is that the woman continues the changes she has implemented in her own behavior.

Begging at the Table

This is an owner-induced problem, period. The solution is simple. The problem starts when you begin feeding the dog at the table, and it ends when you stop feeding the dog at the table.

At my house, even when my dogs get a special tasty treat of some kind, I put it in their dinner bowl. They associate their food with their dinner bowl, and that's the way I like it.

Don't set your dog up for failure. You can't feed him scraps from the table on Mondays and Wednesdays, and then get angry because he's looking for them on Fridays and Sundays. Our dogs are a reflection of us – our consistency or our lack of consistency.

Stealing

We had a Rottweiler for five weeks of in-kennel training recently, and one of the problems his owners had with him was stealing. It seems he had to pass through the laundry room to go from the house to the yard, and en route he loved to steal dirty underwear and socks from the laundry room floor.

He actually was eating some of these things, and the owners knew it was only a matter of time until something was not going to pass through his system and they were going to have a significant medical emergency on their hands.

As problems go, this one was easy.

"You get two laundry baskets," I told them. "You put one on top of the washer, the other on top of the dryer. One is for whites, the other for colored things. The dog won't be able to reach them."

But people are funny. The dog was a bad dog in their eyes, and they wanted the dog to be fixed. As long as they didn't have to play a role in fixing him, it was a dog problem, they maintained, not a people problem.

I decided not to get further involved. Last time I checked, the underwear and socks remained on the floor, and the Rottweiler remained problematic – at least in the eyes of his owners.

And this brings up an important principle in solving problems with canines, and one that I like to adhere to. Keep it simple. Look for the shortest, simplest and most logical route to success, and then follow it. Don't undertake complex and demanding behavior-modification training if some other solution makes more sense.

The dog is tempted by underwear and socks, so let's make the underwear and socks disappear. It seemed simple enough to me.

Lots of dogs like to steal things, by the way. It could be underwear and socks on a laundry room floor or a shoe lying by the front door. A number of things can spark it. One might be competitiveness with the owner. Or it might be attention-getting or game-initiating with the owner or with another dog, or it might involve territorial issues, or perhaps just boredom.

Retrieving breeds often like to have an item simply to carry around in their mouths.

In most cases, the way you deal with the problem is the same. You keep designated items in the house with which the dog can play, such as balls, hard rubber toys and nylon bones. Encourage the dogs to focus on those things and not on your underwear.

Destructive Chewing

One of our clients lived in an apartment above her art gallery, and decided she needed more company in her life, so she obtained a rescue dog from a local animal shelter. The dog was a young one, and hadn't yet had any training. Soon after she obtained him, she decided to leave him in the apartment and go downstairs to the gallery. After all, she wouldn't be far away.

It would have been good if she could have talked it over with the dog, because as far as he was concerned, she might as well have gone to the moon. Gone is gone.

As luck would have it, a week or two before she acquired the dog, this woman acquired a couch. It was a brand new couch made of genuine leather. A very expensive item. Yes, it's like two great story lines coming together in a riveting novel: the dog and the couch. Everyone except the woman knows what's going to happen next.

She returns to the apartment, and the couch no longer is a couch. It's virtually unrecognizable.

Bad dog? Not really, but I wouldn't have wanted to tell the woman that at this moment. The dog behaved quite predictably. Because he was newly adopted, he hadn't had the opportunity to acclimate yet to his new home, his new owner and his new routine. As far as he was concerned, he had been abandoned. He was a high-energy breed, and all of his frustrations were taken out on this couch.

Destructive chewing can occur for any of several reasons. For example a youngster may be teething and feel an instinctive need to chew. Another dog may chew because he's bored. One may be dealing with pent-up stress or excitement, another with nervousness and anxiety.

You control some of these problems through crating, other confinement or constant supervision. If you are unable to supervise, and the dog needs to be alone for a period longer than he can be crated, perhaps he can be confined in a free-standing kennel, where he is safe from the world and the world is safe from him.

A dog needs to be taught how to be alone, and it's a process that requires some time. Start by crating your dog and leaving him alone for a short period say, 10 minutes. After he's comfortable with that, you can extend the time to 20 minutes, then 45 minutes. You are orienting him to the idea of being alone in your living quarters, and by the time you finish the training he will understand that he's not alone forever. You will be back.

Had the woman with the art gallery had the opportunity to do that prior to her dog's first solo home stay, she probably still would have her couch.

Dogs that chew because of stress or excitement, because of anxiety or because of boredom often can benefit from a good physical and mental workout before being left alone. Such a workout could take the form of an obedience exercise, which puts both a dog's mind and his body to work. If your dog is a herding dog, an opportunity to move a flock of sheep, for example, can put him in a whole new frame of mind. A member of a retrieving breed probably would like to run through some retrieving exercises, and if an agility course is handy, a few minutes spent on it can benefit many breeds. Pups that are teething will appreciate safe chewy toys to work on while you're gone.

In a pinch, appropriate confinement always works.

Excessive Vocalization

Vocalizing – barking and whining – is a form of communication and expression for a canine, so it isn't necessarily bad, and it's not reasonable or realistic to think you should correct a dog for all vocalizing. But done to excess, vocalizing can be problematic.

In these cases, you need to work with your dog with leash and collar, since they provide your only ability to telegraph effective messages to the dog. As the dog vocalizes uncontrollably, you should impart moderate snaps of the leash to interrupt the behavior, to register your disapproval of it, and to mark it as undesirable. When he stops vocalizing you should praise him, so you are marking that as well.

A dog that does most of his barking in your absence is harder to deal with, because as a pack leader you can't correct pack behavior when you're not there.

A good place to begin in embracing this type of problem is to determine first of all whether your expectations are in fact reasonable. Some people, for example, turn their dog loose in the yard and then drive downtown, work there all day, and then run a few errands on the way home. They arrive home 12 hours later believing it's reasonable to expect that their dog hasn't been a nuisance to the neighborhood in their absence.

The fact is you may not be able to leave your dog in the yard for 12 hours unsupervised. A free-standing kennel may be your answer to a problem like this. And maybe the best place for that kennel is not in the yard, but in the garage, so if your dog does bark he's not a plague on the entire neighborhood.

Some people opt for the aid of electronic bark monitors to help deal with this problem. They can be helpful, but I would suggest that if you go that route you seek the assistance of a professional in finding the right product and in using it correctly. Some of these products are capable of stimuli that are too harsh, and if you're not familiar with them you may not be aware of what is appropriate.

Some products provide electronic stimulation for correction. Some vibrate for correction, and some spray citronella as a deterrent to barking. Several options are available, and you should have professional advice when you go there.

Other pet owners see doggy day care as a solution to this problem. Many working people bring their dogs to our Stella Ruffington's Doggy Daycare in West Seattle, because they have concluded that they simply can't leave their pet alone all day.

Jumping on People

Dogs jump up on people for a variety of reasons and, especially with larger dogs, people often find it annoying. Dogs that are bullies jump up on people, and also on other dogs. Dogs that are rude or disrespectful jump on people, and dogs that are immature also do it.

However, it doesn't always have to be bad behavior. I invite my dogs to jump up on me at intervals when we're doing obedience work together, as a reward for their hard efforts. But uninvited it would be undesirable behavior, and I would correct them for it.

The way you correct for this is the same way you do for so many things; with training collar and leash. The leash is your telegraph line, and with it you can mark different behaviors.

Commonly, when someone tries to curtail his dog from accosting people at the door of his home, he hollers at the dog from several feet away. But that rarely stops the behavior if the owner hasn't first taught the dog with collar and leash what he wants the dog not to do.

You always should start your training on-leash, whatever it is you want to teach, and your goal is to transfer this new knowledge to off-leash situations as well. So, if you have guests coming to dinner at 6 p.m., at 5 minutes before 6 you should be attaching a leash to your dog's collar so you will be ready when your guests hit the door.

Destructive Digging

Unless there's a varmint lurking in the ground, your dog may be digging out of boredom or frustration. On the other hand, a lot of dogs will dig in the hot summer to lie in the cool earth and help bring their body temperature down.

So you really need to figure out what is motivating your dog's digging. If it's hot, and he's trying to be more comfortable, it's hard to fault him for that. Instead of corrective training or aversion therapy, you might want to find a more comfortable place for him to stay.

If your dog is digging for entertainment, or because of pent-up frustration, an exercise program might help. A dog that is bored or frustrated can be given toys to chew on or given exercise before you leave. But it's a mistake to give him no outlet for his energy.

As a last resort, you can leave your dog in a free-standing kennel so he can't dig up the rest of the yard.

By the way, people often say to me, "Exercise? My dog has a great big yard to around in. He can get all the exercise he wants."

But when is the last time you saw a dog by himself in the corner of a yard doing push-ups or jumping-jacks? Dogs don't operate that way. If you want your dog to have exercise, you have to give him a job to do or a game to play or put him through the paces yourself.

Chapter 18

Dominant Dogs

What counts is not necessarily the size of the dog in the fight; it's the size of the fight in the dog.

— Dwight D. Eisenhower (1890 – 1969)

I hear a lot of people say they have an alpha dog, a "leader dog," and they believe it. Among our clientele, we hear it all the time. Actually, however, many of our clients may never even have seen a truly alpha dog. For the average pet owner, a true alpha would be way more dog than he could handle.

I would estimate that fewer than three percent of the canines that walk the planet are true alphas, and you probably don't rub elbows with them often. A true alpha dog needs to be carefully managed, and so the relationship between dog and owner never will be healthy without work. It never will be maintenance-free. That doesn't mean it can't be rewarding, but the alpha dog will need a higher level of supervision, structure, rules and boundaries than other dogs. And the relationship may carry potential risks.

People sometimes wonder, for example, whether it's okay to have an alpha dog in a home with children. My answer is, not unsupervised, ever. If the dog is a true alpha, it will have the compulsion to correct nearly anything that is out of line. And correction by a canine usually involves teeth. A true alpha often will fight to the point of serious injury – sometimes even to the death – before it walks away from an alpha battle, and it never will decline a fight over status, no matter what the size or strength or ferocity of its opponent.

The larger and more powerful such a dog may be, the higher the probability that the dog can do serious damage. Any potential pet owner who comes into contact with a dog he thinks may be a true alpha needs to make his own assessment of how much potential liability he is willing to assume. It's an individual decision.

If Not an Alpha, Then What?

So, if the dog you thought might be an alpha actually isn't, what might it be, then? Chances are it's what professional trainers and behaviorists call a "dominant" dog. A dominant dog is one with a lot of moxie that often installs himself or herself as boss in a social situation. But that doesn't mean it will be dominant in every situation. For example, a toy breed may be the dominant canine in the environment in which she lives, but she wouldn't necessarily be dominant in other environments. Your dog might be dominant over you, but it might not be dominant over me.

What makes a dog dominant? Often it's the fact that the dog doesn't have an appropriate pack leader at home. If it doesn't, its canine wiring leaves it no choice but to try to assume that leadership role itself.

So what should you do about a dominant dog that may challenge you concerning rank? Is that a problem? It's a problem and a hazard if the dog thinks he's in charge of you. In most cases the problem can be resolved satisfactorily, but I would encourage anyone who believes he has this problem to seek professional assistance. A professional will assess the dog, which often can be done in one 20-minute visit, and will put you on a program that will address the problem.

The professional will use the assessment to determine how pliable the animal is to direction from authority. He will do this primarily by analyzing the animal's body language and reactions to some on-leash psychological pressures, and will evaluate how the animal carries itself, which will tell him how it views its personal stature in the world.

Does dominance always involve aggression on the part of a dog? Normally, yes. Dominance usually will show up first in more subtle behaviors, and if those behaviors are not corrected, the seriousness will escalate. Unfortunately, the early behaviors often are things that the average pet owner doesn't take note of.

Such behaviors may include avoidance of responsibility and authority, noncompliance with simple requests, or the guarding of items or food. Often these things are done so subtly that the pet owner doesn't see the behavior as problematic. If it is not dealt with, however, it normally progresses, and people finally notice the problem when it has risen to the level of aggression.

How can a dog owner become more attuned to this? Simply by following his intuition. He'll often see behaviors that seem out of the ordinary, even a little alarming, but if he hasn't seen a full outburst yet, he might let it slide. Sometimes he just sits on what he's seen until something terrible happens, and that's when he calls our office.

Aggressive Behavior

"Yeah, he was threatening the UPS man, but we never thought he'd actually bite!" is what we often hear.

If you start to wonder if your dog is becoming aggressive, he probably is. Maybe he's barking or growling at people now, or trying to charge at them. Maybe he guards his food bowl or his bones, or guards the home against the meter reader. If you see any of these behaviors, the time for intervention has arrived. It's much easier to cut these behaviors off early than it is to go back and fix things after everything has gone wrong.

Dogs exhibit many different types of aggression, and the proper response to it depends on its type. This is another area where a professional trainer or behaviorist can be of great help, by analyzing both your dog's aggression and the reasons for it, and then providing you with a program for dealing with it. Some dogs, for instance, exhibit aggression that is based in dominance. Others might exhibit:

- Aggression based on possession
- Aggression based on protecting a territory
- Aggression based on prey-drive, which involves stalking, chasing and catching people or animals, often triggered by rapid movement or submissive noises, such as high-pitched squeaks
- Aggression based on fear
- Inter-male aggression, involving mating drive and breeding territory
- Inter-female aggression, involving territorial protection
- Pain-induced aggression, triggered by a sudden and unexpected pain
- Punishment-elicited aggression, developed from intense, harsh punishment
- Maternal aggression, which is defense of puppies a mother feels need protecting
- Redirected aggression, which is what you may have experienced if you tried to break up a dog fight and were bitten by a dog that switched its aggression from the other dog to you.

Analyzing a dog's aggression is not an appropriate job for a novice. But with some professional assistance, it is entirely likely that a novice owner can get the situation headed in the right direction.

A dog that shows any possessiveness at all about its food bowl is some-thing I would act on immediately, especially if I had children or grandchildren in the home. Children must, of course, be taught at an early age to respect animals. We must not allow them to pummel our pets, or to pull ears or to interfere with a dog's dinner, and we must address such behavior immediately, each and every time it occurs. Nevertheless, we cannot allow a dog to launch an attack or a correction because a child has moved his bowl of food. While it's important that we teach our kids respect for animals, as well as boundaries, a child should not be mauled just for being a child in his own home.

Incipient Adulthood

When might you become aware of a potential dominance problem in your household? It can happen after you purchase or adopt a new dog, particularly if that dog is an adult. It also can develop with a dog you have raised since he was a waddler. Dogs progress through stages of life similar to those of people; first infancy, then childhood or puppyhood, then adolescence, then adulthood. When a dog transitions from adolescent to adult, often about the age of 2 ½ to 3, issues sometimes arise. It's a good idea to be aware of this possibility and to continue to be vigilant during this period.

At Camano Island Kennels, we're working now with two separate clients who own young dogs of the same assertive breed. In each case, the pups, each 7 to 9 months old, have been out of control in myriad ways, and I can predict aggression from them with 100 percent certainty by the time they are 2 ½ to 3 years old if they are left to their own devices without human intervention. In each case, the owner is not inclined to take that warning seriously.

Very often, people disregard our warning about young dogs because they don't see the problem with their own eyes. But they're back in our office want-ing to know what they can do about it when the dog has reached mental and sexual maturity and has bitten someone.

Correcting the Problem

You need to establish your leadership with a dominant dog in a non-con-frontational way. You do it with basic leash work, starting with small steps and taking the dog through basic obedience training. You work on skills such as loose-leash walking, sit, stay, down-stay and so forth. This probably will be the dog's introduction to such training because, more than likely, if the dog already has these skills and is comfortable with human leadership, he is not the dog with which you are going to have dominance issues in the first place.

As a trainer, you probably will move a little slower with a dog that thinks it's dominant, applying psychological pressure to him only in smaller-than-usual increments. You first must create a pliable canine mind, and have him open to the idea of taking direction from authority. This again would be a good time to consult a professional to lay out a course of training that proceeds at the right pace for your dog and that uses exercises that are appropriate to reprogram your dog's image of itself and teach it that it is not the leader in your relationship.

Chapter 19

How Much Is Your Dog Worth?

No matter how little money and how few possessions you own, having a dog makes you rich.

— Louis Sabin

A lot of people like to say they've acquired a valuable dog. To some, that's a $500 dog. To some it's a $1,000 dog. To others, it is a dog they love very much.

I know dog-trainer colleagues who have spent in the six figures for a dog. Why, for heaven's sake, would anybody write a six-figure check for a canine? Professional breeders and trainers do it for animals they think will improve their brood stock, for instance, or for animals they plan to train to compete professionally; animals they think might add luster to their own professional reputation.

However, if people spend a lot of money but don't teach their dog rules and boundaries, it doesn't matter what their monetary investment was; their dog may not be worth much. Conversely, people who have acquired a dog for free or for very little money sometimes value it less than they should.

How much is your dog worth? That's a trickier question than it appears to be, because we can assign value to a dog in different ways. For example, dogs have monetary value and dogs have emotional value, and they don't necessarily coincide. Even if we consider only monetary value, we can estimate it by various methods, each of which might produce a significantly different figure.

Let's consider the question from several angles.

In every case, what one pays for a dog is not necessarily what the dog is worth. The dog's monetary value can be significantly higher or lower than its purchase price, depending on the amount of effort and attention that you devote – or fail to devote – to training that animal.

Let me tell you about a talented client of ours who obtained a mixed-breed dog from a local animal shelter after carefully analyzing the personalities of the dogs that the shelter had available for adoption. She thought that the dog she planned to select, a physically nondescript mutt of medium size, offered undiscovered potential. She was right. After bringing the dog home, the woman began a demanding training regimen with it. The dog turned out to be as steady, as intelligent and as willing to please as the woman had thought it would be, and eventually she qualified it for service-dog certification.

For the next several years, that dog took care – *good* care – of the woman's ailing father. It would bring the man's cell phone to him in his recliner, or bring his TV remote, his newspaper, his jacket, whatever he asked for, and would help pull the man out of his recliner when he needed to rise. As a service dog, this animal could go anywhere with the man that the public was allowed to go, including into restaurants, hotels and supermarkets. It would steady the man as he walked, and was a calming influence when the man had anxiety issues.

Eventually, the ailing man passed away, and the dog essentially became unemployed. So the woman who found him at the shelter began to retrain him in service work so that he could detect the effects of a physical ailment and provide the ailing party with assistance if necessary.

The woman acquired this remarkable dog from the shelter for just $75. Amazing? Possibly even more amazing than you might think. Consider this: Other potential adopters had seen the dog at the shelter before she did, and apparently concluded that the dog was not worth $75. Why else would it have been there when she came?

In 2012, when I was considering this dog's story, the woman could have sold him for several thousand dollars to someone with special needs. That was the going price range at that time for a dog with his skills. Such a sale would have provided a profit for the trainer of many times what she had paid. But this was, after all, the dog to which she had safely entrusted her ailing father, and the dog was not for sale at that time at any price.

Emotional attachment and other non-economic factors often play a big part in assessing a canine's value, and they are perfectly legitimate things to consider.

For example, a friend of mine bought a boxer pup for about $650. He was a typical puppy, prone to mischief, and before the age of six months he'd had three intestinal surgeries because of things he'd eaten, such as socks and pieces of shoes. My friend, who was a single, working mother with two boys, spent more than $10,000 on the surgeries and associated care to save the pup's life. A wise decision? Certainly not financially wise. But it was important to her and her family that their puppy be saved and, while she regretted the loss of the money, she never regretted the decision to spend it.

A second example: When my husband served in the military in the Middle East, he often noticed dogs on duty at the gates of American military installations, looking for bombs in vehicles and on the persons of people passing into the installation. The very presence of the dogs at the gates no doubt discouraged bombing attempts, which probably saved lives. How many lives were saved and whose they might have been we only can speculate. But how do you put a monetary value on dogs like those?

Another example: Years ago I took out a personal loan to buy a beautiful young German shepherd dog with good European bloodlines and a tremendous personality. His name was Jago. I was freshly out of a school for dog trainers at the time, and paid $2,700 for Jago, which was a phenomenal amount of money for me then. I took Jago home and put my new dog-training skills to work. Jago soon became a great companion and working dog, and 18 months later a man offered me $10,000 for him. I didn't sell him, because his emotional value to me was far greater than the money. Eventually he died of old age in my care.

So, is it fair to say that Jago was worth $2,700, because that's what I paid for him? Or was he worth $10,000, because that's what somebody offered for him? Or, was he worth more than $10,000, because I declined a $10,000 offer?

One can look at this in any of several ways. But in doing so, don't forget this way, because it's important: If I hadn't employed lots of intensive training to develop Jago's tremendous potential, my $2,700 investment most assuredly would have been worth less, possibly even zero.

We see that phenomenon a lot. Many people who bring their dog to us tell us how much they spent for it, believing the animal to be quite valuable. But sometimes they have done nothing with the dog, and if the foundation of that dog's life has been laid incorrectly it might have little value even as a companion dog. If the situation goes unremedied, it is not likely such a dog could be resold for what its owner paid. In worst-case situations, the owner might not be able to sell it at any price, and might not even be able to give it away.

Chapter 20

Going Forward

Old age means realizing you will never own all the dogs you wanted to.
— Joe Gores

We have come a long way together over the last 19 chapters. I hope you've enjoyed the journey, because I certainly have. I trust that you have gained some insight into how dogs think, and have come away with some idea of how to put that knowledge to work for you.

Now the time has come for you to move on alone, with your dog, and to forge the kind of relationship with him or her that will bring both of you many years of satisfaction.

I have tried to share with you many of the principles I have learned in decades of professional dog training. I have studied under some masters of the craft who shared their insights with me, for which I am grateful, and now I have passed them on to you, along with lessons I have learned in the school of real life. They have stood the test of time.

Here's a thought with which I'd like to leave you: Early in this book, we began to talk about how best to get a point across to a dog in training. The master trainers who instructed me taught me that it was done best with a mixture of rewards and corrections, heavier on the rewards than the corrections. The wisdom of this has been confirmed for me over the course of many years in the dog-training trenches.

In Chapter 9 I talked about various methods of training, and the fact that handlers can choose among several ways to train. I also pointed out that all of these styles work with some degree of efficiency, either more or less, comparatively speaking. Recently, one of these styles has caught a wave of popularity. It involves liberal use of food as a motivator, and shuns the use of corrections.

Both my background and my experience have taught me that a better-balanced approach is more desirable.

Keep in mind that you cannot explain to a dog what you want from him. What you want is a mystery to him at the start of training for any new skill, and it might be helpful to think of this in terms of the "hot and cold" game that you may have played as a child. Do you remember being asked to wait outside a room, at a birthday party, perhaps, while those inside the room hid a small item that you were expected to find when you returned?

When you were readmitted to the room, the others were encouraged to guide you by hollering "hotter" or "colder" from time to time as you moved

about the room trying to determine the location of the treasure. If you got too far off track, the spectators might holler "very cold!" As you got closer to the item, the message would be the opposite.

Now imagine that the "hotter" messages equaled positive reinforcement, awarded when you were moving in the right direction, and the "colder" messages were correctional reinforcement, implemented for moving in the wrong direction.

Finally, imagine that the rules of the game were changed, and the spectators could offer only "hot" or "hotter" messages when you did the right thing, but could provide no information at all to you when you veered off track. Do you think you could have learned the location of the item under those circumstances as quickly as you could have with both types of information being transmitted to you?

A Brief Review

Here are several important principles that you and I have considered already and that you should keep in mind as you move on down the road with your dog. In no particular order, they are these:

- Remember that in every dog-and-handler team, *without exception*, there is a leader and there is a follower. In your dog's eyes you are one or the other. There is no in-between.
- Remember that the best way to assert your leadership is through body language and thoughtful relationship-building.
- Remember that one of the key elements to developing a strong leadership position – so often forgotten – is that in the canine world, a leader always provides pack security in all situations. This means security from perceived dangers on the street and at home that are posed by other dogs, by other people, by wildlife and by apparently threatening inanimate objects. You must step between your dog and the danger that he perceives.
- Remember that it is not good to continue to "rescue" a rescue dog after its rescue is complete. This is the single biggest mistake that some owners make. They sometimes are afraid to demand the kind of behavior from a rescue dog that they would expect from any other dog, fearing that a dog once in need of rescue might be psychologically or emotionally too frail to deal with normal expectations. This invariably has a negative effect on the dog, not a positive one. It transmits to the dog the message that you are not a clearly defined leader, because you don't enforce behavioral standards the way any leader would in the canine world. This robs your dog of a leader when he is most in need of one, and empowers him to make his own decisions, which likely will be poor ones.
- Remember that dogs thrive in a structured environment, and it is up to you to provide that kind of environment. A big part of structure is consistency. Dogs appreciate it. They want to know the rules, and they feel secure when rules are enforced consistently. If you want a dog that is close to 100 percent reliable, then you must provide 100 percent consistency.

• Remember to seek professional advice if you are seriously unsure in any training situation. I have talked about the advisability of seeking input from a canine behaviorist, a trainer or a veterinarian in a variety of scenarios. Remember that there is no shame in this. Even professional trainers and handlers seek input from colleagues or other experts in various circumstances, and find that coaching by another professional can be invaluable at times.

• Remember the importance of socialization in producing a dependable, steady, well-rounded companion dog, especially the socialization that you must provide for him during that critical window of eight to 16 weeks of age. And remember the importance to him of the influence that his mother exerts during the first eight weeks of his life.

• Remember that you must assess your dog to determine what will best inspire him to want to work. You want your dog to be happy and to enjoy working with you.

• Remember the importance of compassion. By its very nature, dog training can be frustrating at times. Sometimes it is a fast process, and sometimes it is a slow one, but it never is a race. We humans live in a world where many of us expect immediate gratification. We won't get it here.

• Finally, remember when working with your dog to use your new understanding of the way dogs think, your empathy and your compassion to appreciate the inherent differences between dogs and people. Try to view situations through your dog's eyes, and expect him to react to things as a canine would and not as a person would. Work with your dog, not against him, for the best training results. In other words, think like your dog and enjoy the rewards.

Index

About the Authors

Dianna M. Young began her dog-training career in Germany, where she served three years of apprenticeship under skilled master trainers, studying and participating in dog training for police-service work, security, scent detection, personal protection, tracking and search-and-rescue.

Dianna returned to the United States and enrolled in a nationally accredited school for professional dog trainers, where she continued her studies in canine behavior, all facets of professional dog training and animal husbandry. Upon completing her schooling, she worked and studied for several years in animal-related fields in New York state. Dianna also served as an Animal Control Officer, enforcing animal-related laws and ordinances in New York state, and managed a 103-animal-capacity shelter and holding facility for a New York township.

Dianna M. Young

Dianna then apprenticed under world-renowned Certified Master Trainer John M. Henkel of New Milford, Connecticut. While employed at the Henkel teaching and training facility, Dianna assisted John with classes for the personnel of many law-enforcement and security agencies in New York and New England, and also with providing trained dogs world-wide to celebrities and dignitaries for personal and estate protection.

After returning to her native Pacific Northwest, Dianna began her own consulting and training services, and spent two years as canine-behavior consultant and in-store dog trainer for outlets of a national pet-supply store chain in two Washington cities.

In 1997 Dianna opened her own training and boarding facility, Camano Island Kennels, where she trains dogs successfully for a wide range of clients. People come to her with needs that range from simple obedience training to the finding and implementing of solutions for complex behavioral problems. She is a first-choice for some veterinarians who seek training for themselves and their own dogs, and teaches classes and seminars in dog-handling for the staffs of veterinary hospitals, animal shelters and rescue organizations.

Since moving to Camano Island, Dianna also has competed successfully at the international level with her own personal service dogs. Some have ranked very high for training in national and international Sieger shows, in which dogs demonstrate proficiency with skills similar to those used by police-service dogs. This has included attaining the position of number-one dog in the United States and number-one dog in Canada in their respective classes.

Robert H. Mottram is an award-winning writer who spent more than 40 years in daily journalism as an Associated Press Correspondent, newspaper reporter, feature writer, columnist and editorial writer. He served for 24 years as outdoor writer for *The News Tribune* of Tacoma, Washington, and is former president and chairman of the board of the Northwest Outdoor Writers Association.

Robert also is author of *Saltwater Salmon Angling*, published by Frank Amato Publications; *Angler's Guide to the West Coast: Salmon and Tuna*, published by Wilderness Adventures Press; and *In Search of America's Heartbeat: Twelve Months on the Road*, a personal memoir about a year on the road in search of the essence of America. He is a recipient of more than 40 national and regional awards for reporting and writing, including two national "Best of the Best" awards for feature writing.

Robert H. Mottram
(Photo by Karen Mottram).